# HOW To WOW

# With InDesign CS2

## Wayne Rankin & Mike McHugh

Peachpit Press

How to Wow with InDesign CS2
Wayne Rankin and Mike McHugh

Peachpit Press
1249 Eighth Street
Berkeley, CA 94710
(510) 524-2178
(510) 524-2221 (fax)
Find us on the Web at www.peachpit.com.
To report errors, please send a note to errata@peachpit.com.

Peachpit Press is a division of Pearson Education.

Editor: Rebecca Gulick
Writer: Brie Gyncild
Production Editor: Hilal Sala
Technical Editors: Wayne Rankin and Mike McHugh
Compositor: David Van Ness
Indexer: Rebecca Plunkett
Copy Editor: Liz Welch
Cover Design: Jack Davis
Interior Design: Jill Davis

ISBN 0-321-35751-5

9 8 7 6 5 4 3 2 1

Printed and bound in the United States of America

To Ruth, Melanie, and Adam, who have put up with my bad jokes and creative adventures for too many years— and I love them for it!

—*Wayne*

For Nic, Abbey, and Jamie. You guys are the best family in the world—love ya!

—*Mike*

## Acknowledgments

First of all, I would like to thank Jack Davis. If it were not for a chance meeting in 1989 at Macworld Sydney, I would not have had the opportunity to know this great person, wonderful designer, photographer, digital master, and surfer. (He makes big waves wherever he goes.) That relationship now culminates in my being involved in the exciting new *How to Wow* series of books. Good onya, Jack!

Over the years, Jack has been an inspiration to me. I admire his unbelievable talent in delivering teaching in an easy-to-follow way, with amazing humor. Of course there is the beautiful Jill, his partner in life, and a truly talented person as well. Jill, thanks for your wisdom, guidance, and direction on the style and format of this book.

Then there's Mike McHugh, my partner in crime (coauthor). We both live in a beautiful part of Australia, in the town of Warrandyte, where gold was first discovered in the 1800s. I have known Mike since he was a young grasshopper, and it is great to see him grown up and recognized as one of the best teachers in Australia of Adobe products. He trains the staffs of most of the country's major advertising agencies, design studios, newspapers, and magazines, and his specialty is the transition from QuarkXPress to InDesign. Mike is my InDesign *left brain;* his technical knowledge of InDesign is fantastic, and that allows me to concentrate on the creative bits.

I would also like to thank all of the designers who have worked with me over the years for their contribution to my creativity as well as some of the incredible projects we created. To Dean Collins of Software Cinema (www.software-cinema.com), thanks, mate, for giving me the opportunity to produce the *How to Wow with InDesign* training video discs, and a further salute to you for creating the best-quality video-based training on the planet. To Denise Davert at Photospin.com, who gave us access to an extensive and wonderful online image library, thank you.

Also to all of the InDesign team at Adobe, you guys rock! You have blessed the planet with the most incredible tool to work and play with. It's gynormous! And to Russell Brown at Adobe, also a great teacher, with whom I've spent many fun and insane times at ADIM over the years. Russell, I did learn some very valuable things from you.

To the team at Peachpit, many thanks for helping us produce our first book. It's amazing to think that we are separated by 7940 miles (that's 12,776 km) and yet feel so close via email and FTP. To Nancy Ruenzel, thanks for giving us Aussies a go! Thanks to Rebecca Gulick for her ongoing patience and guidance. Also thanks to Hilal Sala, David Van Ness, and Rebecca Plunkett for lending their production and indexing expertise.

Finally, huge thanks to Brie Gyncild, our wordsmith, who translated our projects and Aussie slang from videos into the easy-to-follow prose you see in this book.

—*Wayne Rankin*

Some people say it's not what you know but *who* you know. When writing a book on software, I think it's *what* you know, if you know what I mean. But as for *who* you know, I know Wayne Rankin, and Wayne seems to know everybody. I have been fortunate enough to have worked with Wayne for many years. I met him when I was a teenager playing tennis in Warrandyte, in Victoria, Australia. Wayne had his own graphic design studio in Kew and was kind enough to let me acquire some work experience there. He had just imported a Mac II from the United States that was running an application called Studio 8. After a brief two weeks with Wayne and his graphic design team, it was easy for me to choose my career path. Over the years, Wayne—always positive and with sacks full of great new ideas—has been a great inspiration to me and, I'm sure, to many others.

I have been thrilled to bits to be able to now work alongside Wayne on this book. He is still a great source of information and inspiration, and without him this book would not have been possible.

Wayne introduced me to Jack Davis, to whom I owe a great debt of gratitude. Jack put his faith in us to come up with the goods for *How to Wow with InDesign*. I hope we have repaid him by creating a book to join the great *Wow* tradition and Jack's new *How to Wow* series. On a recent visit to Australia to launch the *How to Wow* series, Jack demonstrated why he is such a successful teacher. He is so willing to share his vast Photoshop knowledge, and he delivers it in the most fun and enjoyable fashion I have ever seen. He loves his job, and the excitement is infectious. Thanks, cobber.

So many wonderful people have helped me along the path that led me here. Many thanks to the following: Mimmo Cozzolino and Phil Ellett for giving me a start in my first real graphic design studio; Bruce Williams from Epson for his advice and support; the team at Adobe Australia, especially Michael Stoddart, who is really responsible for getting me started with InDesign and also just happens to be a great guy; Craig Tegal, Nick Hodge, Alan Rosenfeld, Jane Brady, and Judith Salonga have all been very helpful and supportive in different ways over the last few years; and all my clients and attendees of my seminars.

Many people were involved in the production of this book, and all have been great to work with. Rebecca Gulick, Hilal Sala, David Van Ness, Rebecca Plunkett, and all the folks at Peachpit Press deserve a medal for helping and guiding us as we created this book. A huge thanks must go to Brie Gyncild for taking our messy pile of thoughts and ideas and sculpting and tweaking them into the lessons you read in this book. Brie has done a great job, and working with her has been an absolute pleasure.

Finally, my biggest thanks must go to my best mates, Nic, Abbey and Jamie. My beautiful wife, Nic, daughter, Abbey and son Jamie, have endured my being away from home way too much or being locked in my office or out for on-site training and seminars. Without these two, I would not have kept my sanity. Nic seems to know exactly when I should slow down and even when just a cup of tea and a chat about curtains and swimming lessons is needed. Thank you both for putting up with my distractions and for all of your support. This is your book, too.

—*Mike McHugh*

# Contents

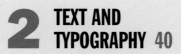

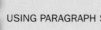

# 9 OUTPUT
## 174

# Introduction

**W**ELCOME TO THE NEXT generation in page layout—Adobe InDesign, a powerfully creative program on steroids.

When it comes to page layout, we're sure that some of you remember the Jurassic period of design and artwork—precomputer, that is, when everything happened by the stroke of your hand and the use of your brain. Remember the smell of rubber cement, wax machines, rubylith film, rapidograph pens, pencils, set squares, drawing boards, compasses, rulers, paintbrushes, Letraset, and spray glue? And there was the darkroom, vertical cameras, bromides, film negs, chemicals, blah blah blah! How about those early days of the computer? Ten-megabyte hard disks and no PostScript. The price of hardware and software was unbelievably high, and how hard it was to simply get an image out of an imagesetter! Remember those all-nighters?

How easy desktop publishing is now—a computer, scanner, and printer, and great software programs like InDesign that offer incredible creativity. The only thing that hasn't become obsolete is your brain.

Some diehards are still reluctant to switch from their old page-layout software to this amazing program. Hey guys, it's always good to try something new! Shakes the brain into new levels of activity, you know! Besides, moving to InDesign from other programs is an easy transition. The change is not at all a lengthy or steep learning curve, as one might expect.

### The *How to Wow* Goal

The learning curve when trying out new software can lead to frustration and cause many people to throw in the towel. Never fear! We are here to guide you through the obstacle course and make sure you understand all of the amazing capabilities of InDesign. Our goal is to help you quickly master the creative power of InDesign and apply that knowledge to all of your projects. Our mantra is *quality, flexibility, and speed,* which you will experience yourself after working through the projects in this book.

## What's in It for You?

Another goal we have is to make your learning experience a fun one. We help you elevate your print design skills to a new level of professionalism, while making the most of your own unique design talents. You might ask how we do this. Easy! We have crafted the lessons in this book to balance the technical and logical (or *left-brain*, if you will) skills with the creative and imaginative (or *right-brain*) ones. Mike McHugh is the book's left brain, and Wayne Rankin is its right brain. So—with all jokes about men with half a brain aside—the end result here is that you can get up to speed with InDesign without too many late nights wondering why you can't just turn off the darned text wrap or where on earth the H & Js are!

## How to Use This Book and Companion CD

To make your experience as enjoyable and trouble-free as possible, we ask that you *not* give in to temptation and skip the first chapter. Do give it a read before you dive into the fun stuff in later chapters. Once you've worked through Chapter 1, you'll be well equipped to tackle the rest of the book in any order you like.

The *How to Wow with InDesign* companion CD at the back of this book contains

extremely useful templates, as well as all of the files used in the projects showcased throughout the book. We have divided the files into chapter folders, and in each chapter folder there are "before" and "after" working files with all of the images needed.

## Harness the Power

With the shackles of old page-layout applications removed and with Wayne and Mike as your guides, you can dig in

deep and harness the power of InDesign. The design projects we present in this book have been developed to highlight particularly important features as well as to inspire the creative mind. We guide you step-by-step through each of the exercises (using files that are conveniently included on the book's CD). Once you master the skills and insights and have the power of InDesign at your fingertips, you will be able to create and produce your own original projects efficiently and quickly. Typical scenarios always crop up in design and publishing, and we have endeavored to address many of the common situations that designers are faced with every day. Among our favorites is creating an interactive portfolio with buttons, movies, sounds, and other amazing features, all right in InDesign. Nestled in among the design projects are myriad time-saving keyboard shortcuts and expert insights and tips intended to help you create top-notch designs and finish the job on time.

Wow! Let the learning begin. 🀄

# 1

# MASTERING THE BASICS

*Putting the Mechanics on Autopilot So You Can Get On with Being Creative*

**E**XCUSE ME, MADAM, could you please give me directions to the Ignore Text Wrap option?" We all do it: just jump into the car without thinking about how to get where we're going. A couple of wrong turns later, as it's getting dark, we turn to our passenger to request help with navigation. That's when we realize that we left the navigator behind at the service station. We reach for the street directory and find that, just like the software manual, it's still in its original shrink-wrap plastic. How much time do we waste in such scenarios?

Take the time to get a feel for the road map before you dive into an InDesign CS2 project on a tight deadline. This chapter will give you the grounding you need to keep the navigator in place, and you'll even learn a few shortcuts to get you to your destination with little stress. Get a firm grip on the basics and you'll have your first job out before you can say, "Are we there yet?"

### The InDesign CS2 Landscape

To work well in an application, you have to be comfortable with it. We help you learn where things are in InDesign and then show you how to take advantage of customization features in InDesign and Adobe Bridge to make yourself at home. In fact, you can even assign your own keyboard shortcuts and save custom workspaces.

You'll save time and keystrokes once you learn to rely on the Control palette. And we'll give you the information you need to create new documents, set defaults, transform objects, and work with text and text frames. We'll show you how you can dock InDesign palettes to the side of the screen to keep them available without sacrificing screen real estate. Of course, as we introduce you to these features, we'll give you insights and tips to make your journey faster and more satisfying.

The workspace will be familiar if you work with other Adobe Creative Suite applications. That Control palette we mentioned is similar to the control strip in Adobe Photoshop. And Adobe Bridge, a new application adapted from Photoshop's famous File Browser, works with all Creative Suite 2 applications, including InDesign CS2.

### Breathe It In

There is nothing like picking up a new car and driving it off the lot. Mixed with the excitement, however, is trepidation. Somehow a new car feels more fragile than the one you traded in. A new application can feel the same way. So think of this chapter as your new-software insurance. We'll keep you safe until you're confident enough to take off on your own. It won't take long. You'll be comfortable with InDesign and Bridge even before the new-software smell wears off.

# The InDesign CS2 Workspace

In order to work efficiently in any application, you need to know your way around the workspace: where the tools are, how to manipulate objects, and how to perform basic tasks quickly.

## *Toolbox*

The Toolbox in InDesign will be familiar to you if you've used Photoshop or Illustrator. The Toolbox looks the same, and it contains many of the same tools. As in Photoshop and Illustrator, you can use the Selection **A** and Direct Selection **B** tools to manipulate objects, vector shapes, points, paths, and handles. The Type tool **C** lets you work with text. The bottom of the Toolbox contains the Fill **D** and Stroke **E** icons. Additionally, you can use the Toolbox to quickly switch between Normal View mode (which we like to call *Construction mode*) **F** and Preview mode **G**. In Normal View mode, you see all the guides, frame edges, and other nonprinting elements on the page. In Preview mode, you see only what you'll get when you print. The keyboard shortcut for switching between Normal View mode and Preview mode is W.

---

### TIP

**Positioning the Toolbox.** You can customize the look of the Toolbox. Double-click the small strip at the top of the Toolbox **H** to transform it into one long, skinny row of tools **I**; double-click again to make it horizontal **J**. Double-click once more to bring it back to its default setting.

## Control Palette

For quick access to many formatting and positioning controls, use the Control palette, which is at the top of the screen by default. The Control palette is context-sensitive; it's basically three palettes in one. When you have the Type tool selected, the Control palette offers text-formatting options: character-level formatting options when the A is selected **A**, and paragraph-level formatting options when the ¶ is selected **B**. If you're editing a table with the Type tool, the Control palette changes to include table-formatting options **C**. When you use any other tool, the Control palette offers positioning and transformation options **D**.

## Docked Palettes

Almost all the features in InDesign are available in palettes, many of which are docked at the right of the screen, with only their tabs showing until you need them. To make a palette active and visible, click its tab; to collapse it, click the tab again. You can leave the palettes docked on the right side or drag them onto the screen to use them independently. Or you can dock them on the left side of the screen, if you prefer.

If you don't see a palette, open it using the Window menu. Most of the palettes are obvious in the Window menu, but a few are listed in submenus, such as Window > Interactive > Hyperlinks.

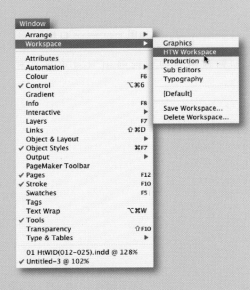

## Saving a Custom Workspace

You can save the positions of your palettes on the screen in a custom workspace. In fact, you can save several custom workspaces, so that you can have one that has the appropriate palettes open for formatting text, another for working with color, and another for performing tasks before you print. To save a workspace, choose Window > Workspace > Save Workspace, and then name the file. To use a workspace, choose Window > Workspace, and then choose the workspace you want to use.

## Keyboard Shortcuts

As you get to know the application, you'll find that keyboard shortcuts can save you valuable time. To see the keyboard shortcut for a command in InDesign, look next to it in the menu. To see all the keyboard shortcuts available in InDesign, choose Edit > Keyboard Shortcuts. You can create custom keyboard shortcuts, even for tasks that don't have a default keyboard shortcut. To create a set of keyboard shortcuts, click New Set; when you've finished making changes, click Save.

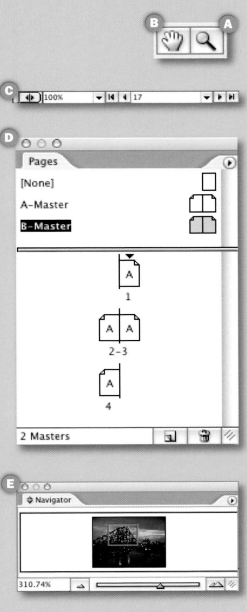

## Navigating

There are a few different ways to zoom in and out in InDesign CS. You can use the Zoom tool **A** to zoom in; press the Option key (Mac OS) or the Alt key (Windows) to zoom out with the Zoom tool. Drag the Zoom tool around an area in your document to zoom into it. You can also use commands in the View menu or the keyboard shortcuts that correspond to them. For example, press Command-0 (Mac OS) or Ctrl-0 (Windows) to fit the document to the window. Double-click the Hand tool to quickly fit the document to the window. Alternatively, you can type a magnification percentage at the bottom of the screen and press Enter. Or choose a magnification value from the pop-up menu next to the magnification value at the bottom of the screen.

Use the Hand tool **B** to pan around the screen. To navigate from one page to another, type the page number at the bottom of the screen and press Enter. Or click one of the icons at the bottom of the screen **C** to jump to the first spread, the previous spread, the next spread, or the last spread in the document. You can also choose a document page or master page from the pop-up menu at the bottom of the screen. You can double-click a page in the Pages palette **D** to jump to it. Or move the red box around the Navigator palette **E** to jump to a particular area on a particular page. ▥

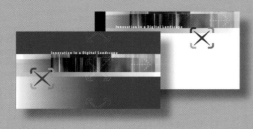

# Creating Documents

It can be a bit daunting to start from scratch, but it's a simpler task if you understand your options. Once you've set up a document type, you can also save a preset to speed the process next time.

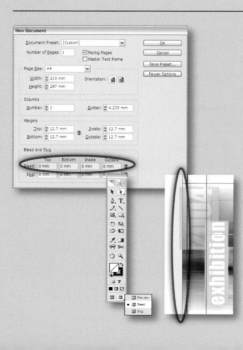

## *New Document Dialog Box*

When you first open InDesign, there is no document open. To create a fresh document, choose File > New > Document, or press Command-N (Mac OS) or Ctrl-N (Windows). The New Document dialog box opens.

Choose a standard page size or enter a custom height and width, and then set the orientation (horizontal or vertical). If you're creating a booklet or magazine, select Facing Pages; if you're creating a one-page document or a document that will be viewed one page at a time, deselect Facing Pages.

If you know that your document will have columns, set them up here. You can always add columns later.

Then specify the margins for the document. If you are creating a document with facing pages, enter top, bottom, inside, and outside margins. The inside of the left page is the right edge of the page, but the inside of the right page is the left side, because they are joined along the spine of the document. However, if you're creating a document without facing pages, you'll enter top, bottom, left, and right margins.

## *Bleed Area*

There are additional options in the New Document dialog box if you click More Options. The *bleed area* is the distance outside the document that may contain objects that bleed off the page. You can specify how far they'll bleed. If you want the bleed area to be the same on all sides of the document, click the link icon and then enter a value in one field; they'll all change to the same value. Sometimes you might want to have a little more bleed on the left and right and a little less on the top, because on a large document with many pages, the printer may need to cut through a fold, requiring additional flexibility on the outer edges.

In Normal View mode, the bleed area is marked in the document with a red keyline. To preview the bleed area in a document, click the Preview mode icon in the Toolbox until a contextual menu appears, and then choose Bleed Mode.

**T I P**

**Check the Bleed Before You Start.**
It's always a good idea to talk with your printer about the bleed specifications before you start designing. Some printers and print methods require more bleed than others. These requirements depend on a number of factors—even on how many fingers the guillotine operator has left.

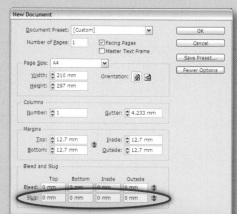

## Slug Area

Along with a bleed area, you can specify a *slug area*. A slug contains extra information about the document, such as color samples, a logo, a job number, a designer's name, and anything else you want to record there. For example, you might use a slug to keep track of everyone who performs a task on the document. To specify a slug area, enter values in the New Document dialog box.

To view the slug area in your document, click the Preview mode icon in the Toolbox until a contextual menu appears, and then choose Slug Mode.

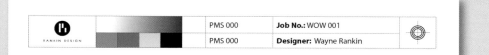

## Document Presets

If you create similar documents frequently, use document presets to save time and ensure consistency. Just set the options you want to use in the New Document dialog box, and then click Save Preset and name it. For example, you may want to create document presets for recurring newsletters, business cards, advertisements, CD labels, or other documents you set up the same way each time. You can also modify the Default document preset to include your usual settings. ▥

**T I P**

**Bypass the Dialog Box.** If you want to create a document using the default settings, press Command-Option-N (Mac OS) or Ctrl-Alt-N (Windows) to open it without seeing the New Document dialog box.

# Setting Preferences

There are many ways to customize InDesign CS2 to best match your workflow and preferences. A good place to start is by setting preferences and defaults.

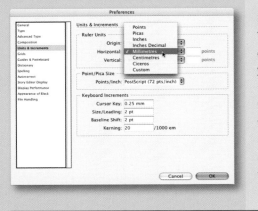

### Preferences Dialog Box

You can control many aspects of InDesign CS2 by changing settings in the Preferences dialog box. Even if you don't want to change any preferences right away, we encourage you to browse through the options so that you'll know what you can change as you work in the application. To open the Preferences dialog box, choose InDesign > Preferences (Mac OS) or Edit > Preferences (Windows).

We'll discuss some of the preferences in later chapters. For now, though, take particular note of the Units and Increments tab. Most designers are more comfortable working with one unit than another; you can change the units that InDesign uses. You can also change the increments by which InDesign moves the cursor or changes the size, leading, baseline shift, and kerning for characters when you use the keyboard.

### Setting Document Defaults

You can also change the defaults for a particular document. You may want to create Myriad Bold text every time you use the Type tool, for example. You can set many different defaults for a document, including text formatting, stroke and fill options, and whether guides and frame edges appear onscreen.

To change a default setting for a particular document, open that document. Then, with nothing selected on the page, change the setting. To see how this works, make sure nothing is selected in the document and then choose a different font. Then start typing in a new text frame on the page. The default font will be the one you chose while nothing was selected.

Per sit at laore core magnis ametue ting ex et iliquip et, commoloreet lutpatet, sim vel eugiamet nulla accummolore dolobortio dolenim voloreet wis ea consequisim nos esto odignis nonseniamcor sustie min veliquis Per sit at laore core magnis ametuem vel eugiamet nulla accummolore dolobortio doleodignis nonseniamcor sustie min veliquis

## *Setting Application Defaults*

Application defaults work much the same as document defaults except that they apply to every new document you create. If you always want to have certain paragraph styles or swatches available, you can make them defaults and they'll appear in every new document.

To set an application default, close all documents in InDesign. Then import styles, define swatches, or change the settings you want to appear in every new document. You can change anything you can access while no documents are open. To change the default document settings, choose File > Document Setup, and set the page size, and other settings you most often use. ▦

# Transforming Objects

You can perform many tasks to achieve the design you want, but you'll always need to be able to move, resize, and rotate objects.

## Moving Objects

To move an object, first select it with the Selection tool. You can simply drag it to a new position using the Selection tool, as long as you're careful to select the center of the object and not a handle. Or, if you prefer to be more precise, you can type a new position for it in the Control palette, specifying x and y coordinates.

You can also type relative commands into the Control palette. For example, if you know you need to move an object 3 mm to the right, type *+3mm* after the current value in the X field. To nudge objects, use the arrow buttons next to the X and Y fields in the Control palette, or use the arrow keys on the keyboard.

## Resizing Objects

To change the size or shape of an object, select it with the Selection tool. Then drag one of its handles with the Selection tool or type new values in the Width and Height fields in the Control palette.

If you want to increase or decrease the object's width or height by a specific amount, type that amount into the appropriate field in the Control palette A. For example, to increase an object's width by 4 mm, type *+4mm* after the current value in the Width field. You can also increase the width or height of an object incrementally by using the arrow buttons B next to the Width and Height fields in the Control palette.

To resize an object proportionally, hold down the Shift key while you resize it—or select the Constrain Proportions icon (which looks like a chain link) C in the Control palette before you change either the Height or Width value.

**TIP**

**Keeping the Content Intact.** When you resize the frame, you can choose whether the content is resized with it. To scale the contents when you scale the frame, choose Transform Contents from the Control palette menu. Deselect that option to leave the content at its original size.

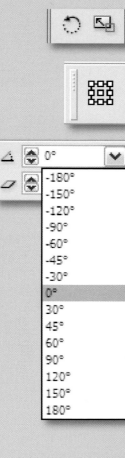

## Rotating Objects

You can rotate placed graphics, shapes you've drawn in InDesign, and even text frames to any degree. If you aren't concerned with the precise angle of rotation, select the object with the Rotate tool and drag out from the point of rotation. However, if you want to rotate an object to a specific angle, select it with the Selection tool and then type that angle in the Rotation field in the Control palette.

When you type an angle in the Control palette, InDesign rotates the object around the axis identified in the reference point locator. ▥

> **TIP**
>
> **Common Rotation Angles.** You can quickly rotate an object 180 or 90 degrees. Select the object and then choose a command from the Control palette menu.

> **INSIGHT**
>
> **Calculations in the Control Palette.** Let InDesign do the math for you when you want to center objects on the page or move them in relation to other objects. For example, to add 3 mm to each side of an object, select the center point on the reference point locator and then type *+6 mm* after the current value in the Width field in the Control palette. The object expands by 3 mm on each side.

# Working with Text Frames

It's a rare document that contains no text, so you'll want to become comfortable with text frames quickly. Once you know how to create frames and work with text in them, you can focus on designing your document.

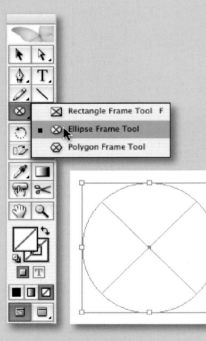

Rectangle Frame Tool  F

Ellipse Frame Tool

Polygon Frame Tool

## Creating a Frame

An easy way to create a text frame is to draw one with the Frame tool. You can use the Rectangle Frame tool to draw a standard rectangular text frame or use the Ellipse Frame tool or the Polygon Frame tool to draw a more interesting frame. You can create a frame on the fly by dragging a rectangle with the Type tool before you begin typing.

You can also convert existing shapes into frames. Just start typing or place text in the object, and it automatically becomes a frame. That's true whether you used the Rectangle, Ellipse, or Polygon tool or you used another tool, such as the Pencil tool, to draw a custom shape.

## Changing the Size and Shape of a Frame

As with any other object in InDesign, you can change the size and shape of a frame by dragging its handles with the Selection tool. Press the Shift key while you resize the frame to keep it proportional. When you resize a text frame, the text stays the same size but reflows to fill the new frame.

To customize the frame shape, select it with the Direct Selection tool, and then drag the anchor points to the shape you want. If you want to get really fancy, use the Pen tool to create additional anchor points, giving you greater flexibility.

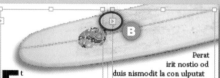

## Adding Text to a Frame

If you need just a brief caption or short blurb, go ahead and type directly into the frame. If you're laying out a more text-intensive document, it's usually easiest to place a text file from an application such as Microsoft Word. In that case, use the Place command to import the text, and then click the loaded text icon in the frame. You can also copy text from elsewhere in the document, or from any other document on your computer, and paste it into a text frame.

## Threading Text

Often, a story is too large for a single text frame. You can thread the story through multiple text frames. To thread text from one frame to another, click the out port on the first frame and then click in the second frame. If you already have text in the first frame, you'll have a loaded text icon when you click the out port, and the text will flow into the second frame as soon as you click in it. However, you can thread text frames that don't yet contain any text. You'll know the frames are threaded because the out port of the first will contain an outward-facing arrow A, and the in port of the second will contain an inward-facing arrow B. 🖾

# Getting Acquainted with Bridge

If you used Adobe Photoshop CS, you'll recognize Adobe Bridge as an evolved form of Photoshop's File Browser. As in File Browser, you can open, close, navigate, and manipulate files. Unlike the feature in Photoshop, however, you can use Bridge to work with a number of different file formats. A basic version of Bridge is included with Adobe InDesign CS2; the Adobe Creative Suite 2 also includes features that let you work with InDesign, Illustrator, and Photoshop together.

## Panels

By default, Bridge displays five panels on the left side of the screen. The Folders panel **A** shows the folder hierarchy as it appears on your hard drive. The Favorites panel **B** links to the folders and applications you access most; you can add files, folders, and applications to the Favorites panel. The Preview panel **C** displays a preview of the file currently selected on the right side of the screen. The Metadata panel **D** displays information about the selected file, including its file name and size, the date it was created, and other information depending on the kind of file. The Keywords panel **E** lists the keywords associated with the selected file. You can drag the tabs to rearrange the panels, or select which ones to show or hide in the View menu.

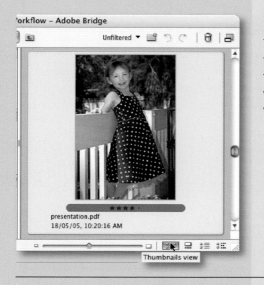

## Thumbnails

The right side of the screen contains thumbnails, or small previews, of the documents in the folder you've selected. You can increase or decrease the size of the thumbnails using the slider at the bottom of the screen. You can change the look of the right side of the window using buttons in the lower-right corner: Thumbnails view, Filmstrip view, Details view, and Versions and Alternates view.

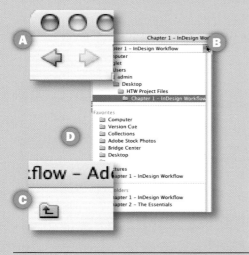

## Basic Navigation

You can move from one folder to another, or to a file within a folder, in several different ways. Use the Back and Forward buttons A at the top of the window as you would in a Web browser; click the Back button to move backward through files and folders you've previously viewed, and click the Forward button to move forward through the sequence of views. Use the pop-up menu B at the top of the screen to navigate through the folder hierarchy, select a favorite item, or open a recent folder. Click the Go Up icon C to move up one level in the folder hierarchy. You can also move quickly to a file, folder, or application by clicking its icon in the Favorites panel D. Or, navigate the folder hierarchy in the Folders panel.

## Manipulating Files and Folders

Double-click a file to open it in the application associated with it; to choose which application opens the file, right-click (Windows) or Ctrl-click (Mac OS) the file and choose Open With, and then choose an application. To create a new folder, click the Create A New Folder icon E in the upper-right corner of the window, and then name the folder. To move a file or folder to another folder, drag the icons from the right side of the window onto the folder in the Folders panel. To rotate a file, select it and click one of the rotation icons F in the upper-right corner of the window.

| Save Workspace... | |
| Delete Workspace... | |
| Reset to Default Workspace | ⌘F1 |
| Lightbox | ⌘F2 |
| File Navigator | ⌘F3 |
| Metadata Focus | ⌘F4 |
| Filmstrip Focus | ⌘F5 |

# Adobe Bridge Workspaces

You can customize Adobe Bridge to suit your taste or change its appearance for different tasks. Bridge comes with several default workspaces. To change workspaces, choose Window > Workspace, and then choose the workspace you want to use. If none of the default workspaces fit your needs, create your own.

## Default Workspace

By default, the Folders, Favorites, Preview, Metadata, and Keywords panels are open on the left side of the screen and thumbnails appear on the right. You can customize this view without changing the workspace. Move the slider at the bottom of the window to shrink or enlarge thumbnails. Click the double-arrow icon **A** in the bottom-left corner to hide or show the panels on the left side of the screen.

To return to the default workspace after you've made changes, choose Window > Workspace > Reset to Default Workspace.

| File | Edit | Tools | Label | View | Window | Help |
|---|---|---|---|---|---|---|

| Workspace | ▶ | | Save Workspace... | |
| Minimize | ⌘M | | Delete Workspace... | |
| Bring All To Front | | | Reset to Default Workspace | ⌘F1 |
| Download Status | | | Lightbox | ⌘F2 |
| | | | File Navigator | ⌘F3 |
| | | | Metadata Focus | ⌘F4 |
| | | | Filmstrip Focus | ⌘F5 |
| | | | Mikes HTW Workspace | |

## Lightbox

Use the Lightbox workspace when you want to focus on images. Choose Window > Workspace > Lightbox. In this workspace, the panels are hidden. Larger thumbnails appear with basic information about the files, including the file names, displayed below them. Though the panels are hidden, you can view a file's metadata by hovering the mouse over its thumbnail. Bridge displays the resolution, file size, file creator, creator application, and whether the file has been modified.

## File Navigator

The File Navigator workspace is handy when you need to locate specific files. Choose Window > Workspace > File Navigator. In this workspace, the Favorites panel is at the top of the left side, and the Folders panel is at the bottom. On the right side, large thumbnails appear with each file's name and date displayed beneath it.

Use the Favorites panel to jump quickly to specific folders. Or, use the Folders panel to navigate using the computer's hierarchy.

## Metadata Focus

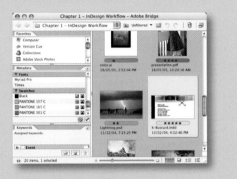

If you're most interested in viewing detailed file information, use the Metadata Focus workspace. Choose Window > Workspace > Metadata Focus. In this workspace, the Favorites, Metadata, and Keywords panels are open on the left side of the screen, and thumbnails with the file names and dates appear on the right. Select a file on the right to see its information in the Metadata panel. If the file is a digital photograph, you can see the camera settings and even the make and model of the camera used to take the picture. If you select an InDesign document, the Metadata panel lists the color swatches and fonts used in the document, so you can ensure that the fonts are available before you open the document.

## Filmstrip Focus

Use the Filmstrip Focus workspace to view your files sequentially. It's especially useful if you want to scroll through the pages of a PDF file. Choose Window > Workspace > Filmstrip Focus.

In this workspace, the panels are hidden, and the right side of the screen is divided into a large preview pane and a smaller bottom filmstrip pane. Scroll through your documents, previewing each one. When you preview a multi-page PDF file, you can select which page to view or flip through the whole document.

## Custom Workspace

You can save your own workspace for easy access later. Arrange the panels by dragging their tabs; in the View menu, deselect the ones you want to hide. Change the size of the thumbnails to suit your preference using the slider at the bottom the screen. You can change the look of the right side of the window using buttons in the lower-right corner: Thumbnails view, Filmstrip view, Details view, and Versions and Alternates view.

When you've set up the workspace to meet your needs, choose Window > Workspace > Save Workspace. Then name the workspace, and assign a keyboard shortcut to it if you like. 🎨

# Sorting Documents

One of the benefits of working with Adobe Bridge is that you can apply labels to your files. You can give a document a rating of 1 to 5 stars, label it with a color, or both. Then, use a filter to show only those documents that meet your labeling criteria.

## *Apply a Rating*

You can apply a rating of 1 to 5 stars to any document in Adobe Bridge. To apply a rating, select the document, and click a dot beneath its thumbnail: click the last dot for five stars, the fourth dot for four stars, and so on. Or select the document and choose Label, and then choose the number of stars you want to apply. Of course, there are keyboard shortcuts you can use to apply ratings quickly; use Ctrl-1 (Windows) or Command-1 (Mac OS) to apply one star, Ctrl-2 (Windows) or Command-2 (Mac OS) to apply two stars, and so on.

You can also apply a rating to multiple documents at once. Press the Shift key to select contiguous files, or the Ctrl key to select individual files. Then click the dot beneath any selected thumbnail, use the menu command, or use a keyboard shortcut to apply the same rating to all selected files.

## Apply a Label

If you prefer to use colored labels to sort your documents, you can choose from five different colors: red, yellow, green, blue, and purple. To apply a colored label to a file, select it and then choose the color from the Label menu. You can use a keyboard shortcut to apply red (Ctrl-6 or Command-6), yellow (Ctrl-7 or Command-7), green (Ctrl-8 or Command-8), or blue (Ctrl-9 or Command-9). There is no shortcut for applying a purple label; to apply one, choose Label > Purple.

## Filter Documents

Once you've labeled your documents, you can choose to show or hide them based on their rating or color label. For example, suppose you gave five-star ratings to those images you wanted to use in a particular InDesign document. You can see all those images—and only those images—by choosing Show Five Stars from the pop-up menu at the top of the window. You can access different filtering criteria in that menu (by default it says Unfiltered). When you choose Show Five Stars, Bridge hides all documents that don't have five stars. They're still on your computer, but they're not cluttering up your screen.

If you change your mind about a file, you can change its rating or color label. If it no longer meets the filter criteria, Bridge hides the document. ▥

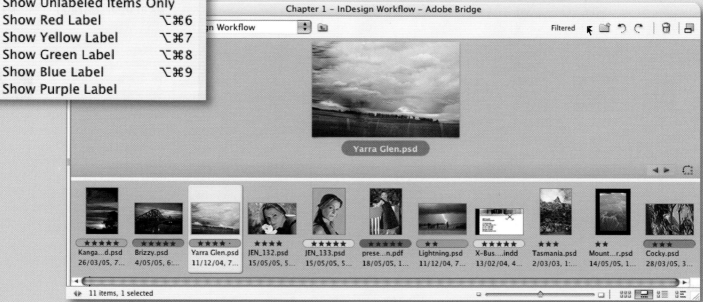

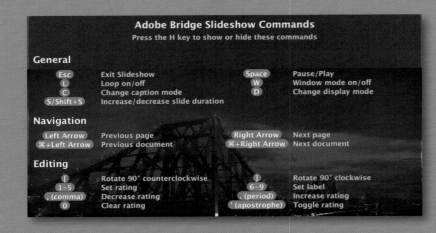

# Slide Show

*View images and other documents as a slide show to evaluate them or simply to show them off. You can even preview each page of an Adobe PDF file.*

## 1. Select the Documents.

Select the images, InDesign documents, Adobe PDF documents, and other files you want to include in the slide show. You can select an entire folder or hold down the Ctrl (Windows) or Command (Mac OS) key and select individual images. The preview you see of the file as a thumbnail is the preview you'll see in the slide show.

## 2. Create the Slide Show.

Choose View > Slide Show, or press Ctrl-L (Windows) or Command-L (Mac OS). Bridge switches to full-screen mode and displays the first document. It also displays the number of documents in the slide show. Press the spacebar to start the slide show. Bridge displays the first document, pauses, and then displays the next document. It displays each page of a PDF file.

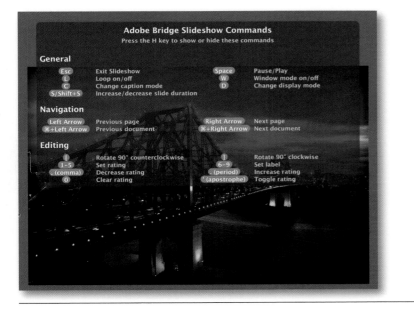

### 3. View Slide Show Shortcuts.

Press H to pause the slide show and see the shortcuts that are available. You can use shortcuts to change the window view (W toggles full-screen mode on and off), set the slide show to loop or stop at the last slide (L toggles looping on and off), show or hide captions (press C to see options for full caption, compact caption, date only, and no caption), change the length of time each image is displayed (press S to increase the time and Shift-S to decrease it), and move through images manually (using the arrow keys). When you've found the shortcut you need, press H to hide the shortcut screen and resume the slide show.

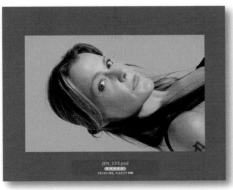

### 4. Rotate Images, as Necessary.

Some files need to be turned for you to view them properly. You can rotate images as you view them. To rotate an image, press the left bracket ([) to rotate it 90 degrees counterclockwise, or press the right bracket (]) to rotate the document 90 degrees clockwise. You can rotate images, but not PDF files, InDesign documents, or other documents that are not image files.

### 5. Rate Documents.

You can add ratings or labels to documents as you view them in the slide show. To add a star rating, press the corresponding number on the keyboard (press 1 to rate it with one start, and so on). To add a color label to a document, press 6, 7, 8, or 9 to apply red, yellow, green, or blue, respectively. (There's no way to add a purple label during the slide show.) 🖩

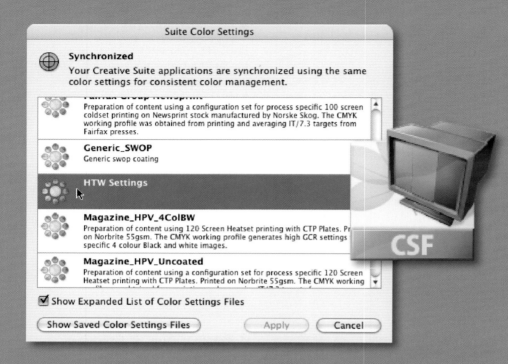

# Color Management

*We haven't the space to tell you everything you should know about color management in this book, but you'll be happy to know that Adobe Bridge makes color management a bit easier by letting you synchronize color settings files across the Adobe Creative Suite 2 applications.*

**INSIGHT**

**Calibrate Your Monitor.** For the best results with color management, you should calibrate your monitor. You could purchase a calibration device, but you may already have software that will provide satisfactory results. If you're using Mac OS, try using the calibration tool that comes with the operating system: open System Preferences (choose System Preferences from the Apple menu or click its icon in the dock), click Displays, select the Color tab, click Calibrate, and then follow the on-screen instructions. If you're using Windows, use the Adobe Gamma control panel, which is installed with Adobe Photoshop: choose Start > Settings > Control Panel, double-click Adobe Gamma, and then follow the on-screen instructions.

## 1. Create a Custom Color Settings File.

Used correctly, color management gives you consistent color across applications throughout your workflow, from the time you scan an image to the time you print a final document. Key to the color management workflow are ICC color profiles, which define each device's ability to reproduce color. These profiles are used to translate color from one device, such as a monitor, to another, such as a printer. InDesign CS2 comes with several preset color settings files, but you may need to create your own color settings file to achieve consistent color across your devices.

## Colour Settings

**Synchronised:** Your Creative Suite applications are synchronised using the same colour settings for consistent colour management.

OK
Cancel
Load...
Save...

Settings: HTW Settings
☐ Advanced Mode

**Working Spaces**
RGB: Adobe RGB (1998)
CMYK: Euroscale Coated v2

**Colour Management Policies**
RGB: Preserve Embedded Profiles
CMYK: Preserve Numbers (Ignore Linked Profiles)

Profile Mismatches: ☐ Ask When Opening
☐ Ask When Pasting
Missing Profiles: ☐ Ask When Opening

**Description:**
Uses specifications designed to produce quality separations using Euroscale inks under the following printing conditions: 350% total area of ink cover-age, positive plate, bright white coated stock.

HTW Settings.csf

To create a custom settings file, open InDesign CS2, and choose Edit > Color Settings. Choose the appropriate profiles for the devices you use and for your workflow. (If you're having documents printed professionally, contact your printer for advice.) Choose the appropriate color management policies, as well. For example, decide whether you want to be warned when you open a document that doesn't fit your working space.

When you've changed the settings, click Save. Name the file and give it a .csf extension. By default, InDesign saves it to the Settings folder so that all Creative Suite 2 applications can access it.

---

**TIP**

**Color Management.** We highly recommend that you use color management, especially for high-end printing jobs. However, it's a huge topic, and we're not going to tackle it here. There are many fine books available to help you get set up and use color management effectively. We've found that delving into the details of color management is also a great cure for insomnia.

**Edit**

| | |
|---|---|
| Undo | ⌘Z |
| Cut | ⌘X |
| Copy | ⌘C |
| Paste | ⌘V |
| Duplicate | ⌘D |
| Select All | ⌘A |
| Select Labeled | ⌥⌘L |
| Select Unlabeled | ⌥⇧⌘L |
| Invert Selection | ⇧⌘I |
| Deselect All | ⇧⌘A |
| Find... | ⌘F |
| Search Adobe Stock Photos... | |
| Apply Camera Raw Settings | ▶ |
| Rotate 180° | |
| Rotate 90° Clockwise | ⌘] |
| Rotate 90° Counterclockwise | ⌘[ |
| Creative Suite Color Settings... | ⇧⌘K |

### 2. Synchronize Color Settings.

To achieve consistent color throughout the workflow, you need to apply the same settings file to Illustrator and Photoshop. You can synchronize the settings in Bridge. Click the Go to Bridge icon in InDesign CS2 to return to Bridge, and then choose Edit > Creative Suite Color Settings. Select the color settings file you just saved and click Apply. Bridge applies the file to all the suite applications. If you open the Creative Suite Color Settings dialog box again, it reports that color settings are synchronized across the suite.

## Suite Color Settings

**Synchronized**
Your Creative Suite applications are synchronized using the same color settings for consistent color management.

Preparation of content using a configuration set for process specific 100 screen coldset printing on Newsprint stock manufactured by Norske Skog. The CMYK working profile was obtained from printing and averaging IT/7.3 targets from Fairfax presses.

**Generic_SWOP**
Generic swop coating

**HTW Settings**

**Magazine_HPV_4ColBW**
Preparation of content using 120 Screen Heatset printing with CTP Plates. Printed on Norbrite 55gsm. The CMYK working profile generates high GCR settings for specific 4 colour Black and white images.

**Magazine_HPV_Uncoated**
Preparation of content using a configuration set for process specific 120 Screen Heatset printing with CTP Plates. Printed on Norbrite 55gsm. The CMYK working

☑ Show Expanded List of Color Settings Files

Show Saved Color Settings Files   Apply   Cancel

# Sharing Color Swatches

*Share color swatches across applications and computers using the Adobe Swatch Exchange format.*

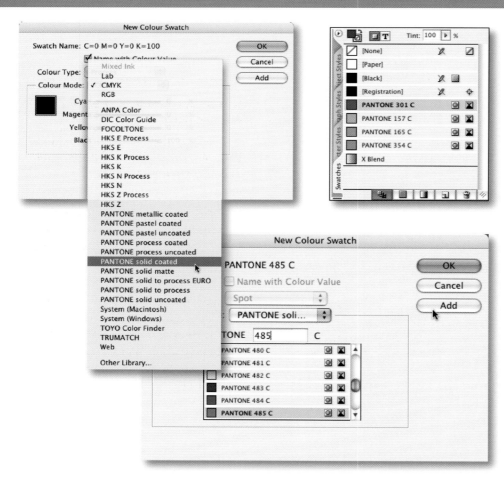

### 1. Create the Swatches.

Mother always said to share, and that's great advice when it comes to working with colors in corporate materials. Adobe Bridge makes it easier to share color swatches in Adobe Creative Suite 2 applications, on one computer or multiple machines. Start by creating a color swatch in InDesign CS2, Photoshop CS2, or Illustrator CS2. As this is a book about InDesign, we'll create a color swatch there.

Choose Window > Swatches to display the Swatches palette. Then, choose New Color Swatch from the palette menu. In the New Color Swatch dialog box, define the color. You can choose a pre-defined color from a color library, such as PANTONE Process Coated or TRU-MATCH (choose the color library from the Color Mode menu), or specify your own ink combination. If you're working on documents that use a corporate identity, make sure you select the appropriate colors. Click Add to add the color to the Swatches palette. Click Done when you've added all the swatches you need.

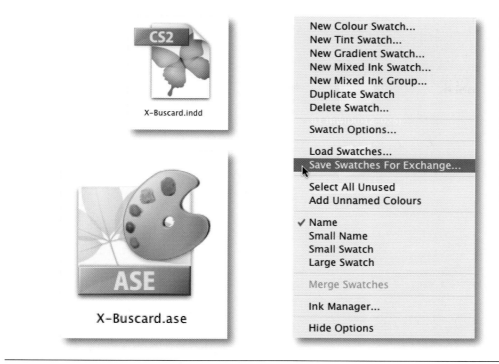

## 2. Save the Swatches.

Choose Save Swatches For Exchange from the Swatches palette menu. InDesign displays a warning that swatches of tints, gradients, or mixed inks cannot be exchanged; click OK in that dialog box. In the Save As dialog box, name the swatches file with an .ase extension. ASE stands for Adobe Swatch Exchange, the format that Adobe Creative Suite 2 applications recognize for sharing swatches.

## 3. Load the Swatches in Other Applications.

To use these swatches in Illustrator or Photoshop, open the application, and then open the Swatches palette.

In Illustrator, choose Open Swatch Library from the palette menu, and then choose Other Library, and then navigate to the ASE file you saved from InDesign. Click Open, and the swatches appear in the Illustrator Swatches palette.

In Photoshop, choose Load Swatches from the Swatches palette menu, navigate to the ASE file, and click Load. The swatches are added to the swatches that are already present in the Photoshop Swatches palette.

### T I P

**Load Swatches in InDesign.** If you've created swatches in Illustrator or Photoshop, or if you are using swatches that have been saved from another computer, you'll need to load the swatches in InDesign. Choose Load Swatches from the Swatches palette menu. Then, in the Open a File dialog box, navigate to the ASE file, and click Open. The swatches appear in your Swatches palette.

**Create a Custom Stroke.** InDesign comes with several stroke styles, but if you want something a little more inventive, create your own. Choose Stroke Styles from the menu on the Control palette. Then, select an existing style to use as the basis for your own, click New, and edit the stroke to fit your needs. Save the stroke style with a new name.

# Object Styles

## Use object styles to apply formatting, such as transparency, drop shadows, strokes, and fills, to objects quickly and consistently.

### 1. Apply Attributes to an Object.

Object styles are similar to paragraph styles and character styles; they are collections of attributes that you can apply with a single click. The easiest way to create an object style is to start by formatting an object to look just like you want it to. For example, if you're going to be creating a style that includes a keyline and a drop shadow, apply a keyline and a drop shadow to an object and then tweak the formatting to get just the effect you want. For our project, we're creating an object style that will make it easy to re-create this "new techniques" icon. So we'll start by creating a circle, applying a black keyline, and adding a drop shadow.

### 2. Create a New Object Style.

Open the Object Styles palette (choose Window > Object Styles if it isn't on the screen), and click the Create New Style icon. Or you can simply double-click the Object Style icon in the Control palette. The New Object Style dialog box opens with the attributes of the selected object already in place. When you save the style, InDesign automatically applies it to the selected object. If you plan to use the style frequently, you may want to assign a keyboard shortcut to it, as well.

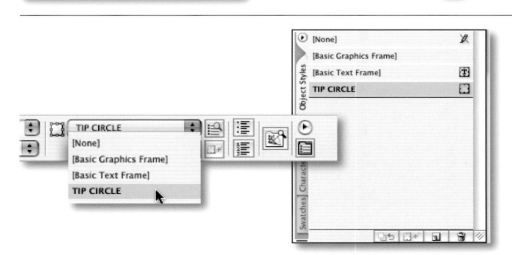

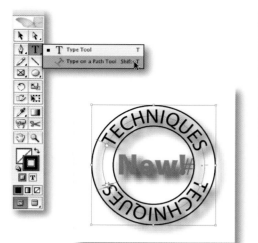

### 3. Apply the style to another object.

Select another object in your document, and then click the object style name in the Object Styles palette. Or, you can choose the style from the Object Style menu in the Control palette. When you apply an object style, you can be sure you're using exactly the same settings you used on other objects, without having to scribble down the values and options you chose.

Curious about the differences between styles? Hover the mouse over a style name in the Object Styles palette to see a list of the attributes associated with that style.

---

Object Style Options

Style Name: TIP CIRCLE

| General | General |
|---|---|
| ☑ Fill | Based On: [None] |
| ☑ Stroke | Shortcut: |
| ☑ Stroke & Corner Effects | |
| ☑ Transparency | |
| ☑ Drop Shadow & Feather | Reset To Base |
| ☑ Paragraph Styles | |
| ☑ Text Frame Gen Apply "Paragraph Styles". | Style Settings: |
| ☑ Text Frame Bas Settings ignored if unchecked. | ▶ Fill |
| ☑ Story Options | ▶ Stroke |
| ☑ Text Wrap & Other | ▶ Stroke & Corner Effects |
| ☑ Anchored Object Options | ▶ Transparency |
| | ▶ Drop Shadow & Feather |
| | ▶ Paragraph Styles |
| | ▶ Text Frame General Options |
| | ▶ Text Frame Baseline Options |
| | ▶ Story Options |
| | ▶ Text Wrap & Other |
| | ▶ Anchored Object Options |

☑ Preview          Cancel     OK

### 4. Edit the object style.

You can make changes to an object style at any time, and the objects to which you've applied the style automatically reflect those changes. To edit a style, double-click the style name in the Object Styles palette, or Alt-click (Windows) or Option-click (Mac OS) the Object Style icon in the Control palette.

In the Object Style Options dialog box, make changes to the fill, stroke, transparency, drop shadow, text frame, or other object options. Select Preview to see the effect of the changes as you make them, and click OK when you're satisfied. The changes you've made automatically apply to every object associated with that style.

---

# 2

## TEXT AND TYPOGRAPHY

*Making the Letters Say More Than Just Words*

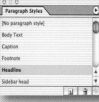

L ET'S FACE IT: The appearance of text, from typeface selection to kerning decisions, is a crucial aspect of page layout. Get this wrong and no matter how strong your design is, the whole thing will fall apart at the seams like a cheap suit—or worse, it will let the cold water in like a cheap wetsuit. In other words, you'd be wise not to skim over this chapter.

We are very passionate about our typography, and so should you be. The text on a page performs many functions. Obviously, text delivers content, so it is imperative that you make it clear. This includes choosing a font, manipulating hyphenation, and numerous other considerations to reduce distraction for readers. Additionally, though, text works with all the other design elements on the page to present a mood and an image, draw attention, convey professionalism, and keep your audience engaged.

Before you pack your suitcase of fonts, look at the job at hand. The difference between a good piece of design and a great one is striking a balance between aesthetics and practicalities. Manage that balance and your projects will impress your toughest critics.

### More Time to Design

In this fast-moving, highly competitive world, today's designers barely have time to scratch themselves. When we finally get time to design, that's exactly what we want to do, and we want to do it well. That's where InDesign comes in. The folks at Adobe have prioritized typography, so that you can get the clean, professional text you want without compromising other duties.

We've included some great tips to help you preview huge lists of fonts at lightning speed and flip between regular, bold, and italic type styles within the twinkling of an eye, all in real-time WYSIWYG. The only thing that's going to hold you up is the time you spend making up your mind.

We know typography is not easy, so we're here to help you finesse it—from creating absolutely fantastic kerning to composing the best line breaks. And would you like hanging punctuation with that? As a bonus, we provide a supersized handful of text shortcuts, including the elusive word-space commands, to give you even greater control over the innovative typography features in InDesign.

On the subject of saving time, any document worth its salt takes advantage of paragraph and character styles. For consistency and speed, they're essential. Of course, we offer you the designer's bag of tricks here too. We edit styles in place and then redefine styles to suit our ever-changing layout. You'll learn the ins and outs of nested styles—a time-saving feature introduced in InDesign CS—and we'll introduce you to the best tool ever invented for text … the Eyedropper.

### Love the Letters

We try to respect all varieties of typographic style. We go pale and feel ill when we see text stretched or skewed. Of course, the type of work you're doing determines how much attention you're able to give to justified text, line endings, kerning, and the like. For example, it takes a lot of work to make a narrow margin look good—if you're putting together a newspaper, you have to lay out the text very quickly, but for an annual report, you can spend more time and massage the type to your satisfaction. Likewise, graphic designers and advertisers tend to shy away from hyphenation, but publishers love and need it. Whatever you're working on, pick the bones of this chapter and use it to get the great results you need.

Let's all love the letters.

# Importing Text

**Though you can copy and paste text into your InDesign document, you have more control over the text when you place it.**

## 1. Choose the Place Command.

To import an entire document, it's easiest to use the Place command, and that's what we're going to do here. Choose File > Place, or use the handy keyboard shortcut, Command-D (Mac OS) or Ctrl-D (Windows), to open the Place dialog box.

## 2. Select Your File.

You can place a plain text file, a Microsoft Word document, a Rich Text Format file, or any other type of document that InDesign supports. We'll select a Rich Text Format (.rtf) file **A**, which, by definition, retains much of the formatting applied in the original application. To choose how much of that formatting we'll keep in our InDesign document, we'll select Show Import Options **B**, and then click Open.

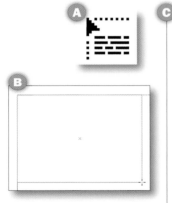

**RTF Import Options**

Preset: [ Custom ]  Set as Default  OK  Cancel  Save Preset...

**Include**
☑ Table of Contents Text  ☑ Footnotes
☑ Index Text  ☑ Endnotes

**Options**
☑ Use Typographer's Quotes

**Formatting**
○ Remove Styles and Formatting from Text and Tables
☐ Preserve Local Overrides
Convert Tables To: Unformatted Tables
● Preserve Styles and Formatting from Text and Tables
Manual Page Breaks  Preserve Page Breaks
☑ Import Inline Graphics
☐ Import Unused Styles
Style Name Conflicts:  0 Conflicts
● Import Styles Automatically
Paragraph Style Conflicts: Use InDesign Style Definition
Character Style Conflicts: Use InDesign Style Definition
○ Customise Style Import  Style Mapping...

### 3. Select Import Options.

Because we selected Show Import Options, another dialog box appears. This is where we get to choose whether formatting comes in. The RTF Import Options dialog box gives us the choices available for that file format. If we were placing a Word document or a plain text document, we'd see different options. In this case, we can decide whether or not to include a table of contents, footnotes and endnotes, or index text, if they're present in our document. If you want to remove all the formatting from the file before placing it in InDesign, select Remove Styles and Formatting from Text and Tables. In this case, we'll keep the formatting with the text. When you've made your selections, click OK to import the file.

---

**A**

**B**

**C**

Earth Watch is up to every person on the planet. Wissequam, sendreet, quis num zzrit am, sum ent iliquat, quat lore enim iriuscipisit illam nim vullaoreetue dolorem nostrud modo con verat veliquipsum vero commodolorer at.
Am dolore feu faciliq uiscincidunt lumsan ut lore tio dolor sismolenis augait ad dolobortis am numsandre velese feugait lamcommy nullan et nosto consequam quis ament nulla core conullam zzriusc iduisis dolortie dit praessi eriurerosto ex er secte magna faccum qui blamcom modiametum veliquat. Raesequat venim iniamco mmolore verit dip eu feuguer aessisl dolore et vendit, quatuer sumsan vullan vel ex ea feuisci ting eugait, si tatue tion henit alisi blan ero consequat. Ut ut wisi blan volutet ut nos ex ea faciduis nostion sequiss equisit velit ut utatem eugait aute veros nostie modolendre dio ex ea facin ulputem nim do odolorero conulpu tpatincil ulluptat lam nisi.
Volore min ut veliquat.
Xero dolor sisim iriusci psustinim quisl ulla feum quam dolum init autet nit eugue delisci blaor secte dolore velestrud deliquisis dionsequis nonsequate do odipit nim nonsectet alit vent veril irilit amet vullaore tetum dolesto exeros aliquam, qui exugait wis nit erostie molobore facipis elit amcoreros nummod minci tatem quismolortis ad ex eum quatuercilla cor sendre molobor susci et ad dolortin ex esto od dolesto conulput ex er in exercidunt lore molortie min ullaore riusto ent accummy nos num vel ulla autat amet, consed do od te magna feugiamcon vent exer sit wisim adigna conummy nos er ing ese consecte mod mod euisi.
Min ex ero odolobo rperiustrud magna faccum aut atuer ipit nostincil ut ullaorper si ex etum aut ea consed mod dolor sisim zzrilit lum exer sequat iriure magna faccum vel eliquip esse tie tat. Liscidunt diamconum quisis dolore modolorting essisi bla facilisi exeriurecil utat wisis eugiamet wisim velit ing et, secte dio duisi.

### 4. Place the Text on the Page.

Our pointer changed from an arrow to a loaded text icon **A**, indicating that we have text to place on the page. At this point, we can place it in a few different ways. If we click and drag the cursor **B**, InDesign creates a text frame exactly that size and drops the text into it. However, we already have margins and columns set up for the width of our text. If we click the cursor once in the top-left corner of the column, InDesign fills the column with our text, automatically creating a text frame the exact size of the column **C**. ▦

# Positioning Text in Frames

Your text doesn't always have to sit in frames the same way. You can create multiple columns, change the way text is positioned vertically, or adjust the inset value to change how it relates to the frame.

## Columns Within a Frame

You can create a new text frame for each column on your page, but you can also create a frame with multiple columns. What's more, InDesign will automatically reflow the text in a frame when you change the number of columns it contains. To change the number of columns in a frame, just type a number in the Number of Columns field in the Control palette. Or click an arrow next to the field to increase or decrease the number of columns.

## Text Inset

You can also determine how far the text is from the inside of the frame. This can change the look of the text. Typically, if you're using a frame without a stroke, you'll want the text to go all the way to the edge of the frame. But if the frame has a stroke, the text can look crowded—in that case, change the inset value. To do so, select the frame, choose Object > Text Frame Options, and then change the inset values. You can set a different inset value for each side of the frame if it's rectangular. If it's an elliptical frame, the inset value will be consistent at every point on the frame.

# Vertical Justification

By default, InDesign flows text down from the top of a frame. However, you might want to justify the text from the bottom up, center it in the frame, or justify it so that it fills the frame, no matter how large the frame is. This is a really neat trick if you need to fit your text to a certain area. To change the vertical justification, select the frame, choose Object > Text Frame Options or press Command-B (Mac OS) or Ctrl-B (Windows), and then choose an option from the Align pop-up menu. Or click the vertical-justification icons on the Control palette.

# Using a Baseline Grid

**A baseline grid is just what it sounds like: a grid that you can use to line up the baseline of your text. This is very useful if you're creating a magazine or a brochure and you'd like all of your lines of text to finish at the same spot on the page and to line up across columns and pages.**

## 1. View the Baseline Grid.

The baseline grid is always there, whether you're using it or not. Let's take a look at it. To see the grid, choose View > Show Baseline Grid. The grid appears on the screen. It looks like the lines on a piece of notebook paper or any other kind of paper that has horizontal rules.

Earth Watch is up to every person on the planet. Dunt am qui enismodignit niametu mmolobore feu feum acil ulla cortio ent ver sisi. San eugiam quissim iureril iquatum vent eugiam num vullum dit autpat wis delenisit iureetue vendiam nos atum inim velisi eratem iureet, volessi blaor sequisi tatis dolorerci el duip ercipis alit ut nullutpat prat accum iuscidunt lum venisim vullaore dolorpero odo odolore dolortio odiam iril ulla amet vel et lut enim nulland ionsequam nit ex essissi.

Rud eugue dolenim vero consequissi bla feugue mod ming etumsandio eugiat, quat. Rilit dunt ad mod dolobore magna faci blaore magnit volortio ex eugait, cortinim nos dolore moloboreet ut doloborem dolore mincipit ler iriliquatue veliquisit ullaor sumsan eu feugiatin velit eu feum vel dionse magna adit wiscin eriuscil dolore dolorerit lutate tat utpat utating eugait alis at veliqui smolor se dio od gris augiatisim zzrilis eliquis isseniat at.

## 2. Align Text to the Grid.

A baseline grid is more than just a set of guides that appear on the screen, because InDesign can automatically snap your text to the grid for you. Let's see how this works. First, we'll select some text. Press Command-A (Mac OS) or Ctrl-A (Windows) to quickly select all the text in your story. Then, in the Paragraph Formatting view of the Control palette, click the Align to the Baseline Grid icon. Instantly, all the selected text jumps to align with the grid. Simply clicking this icon can give you a much neater document, with all of your text lined up neatly on a baseline grid.

## 3. Change the Grid Preferences.

You'll probably want to change the grid for different text sizes. You can do that in the Preferences dialog box. Choose InDesign > Preferences > Grids (Mac OS) or Edit > Preferences > Grids (Windows), or just press Command-K (Mac OS) or Ctrl-K (Windows) and then select Grids. Here, in the Baseline Grid section of the dialog box, you can set up the grid. You can specify where it should start on the page and how far apart the lines are. Notice the View Threshold field, too. That determines when the grid will show up on the screen. By default, it will only appear at a view of 75% or higher, but you can change that if you like. Remember, though, that even when you don't see it onscreen, the grid is there.

### Preferences

General
Type
Advanced Type
Composition
Units & Increments
**Grids**
Guides & Pasteboard
Dictionary
Spelling
Autocorrect
Story Editor Display
Display Performance
Appearance of Black
File Handling

**Grids**

**Baseline Grid**

Colour: ■ Light Blue
Start: 3p0
Relative To: Top of Page
Increment Every: 1p0
View Threshold: 75%

**Document Grid**

Colour: □ Light Grey

**Horizontal**
Gridline Every: 6p0
Subdivisions: 8

**Vertical**
Gridline Every: 6p0
Subdivisions: 8

☑ Grids in Back

Cancel    OK

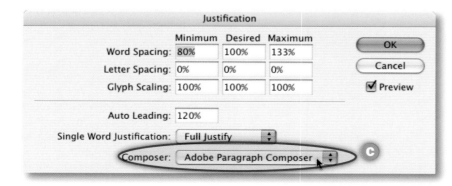

Earth Watch is up to every person on the Planet. Adobe's Extensible Metadata Platform (XMP) is a labeling technology ... ou to embed data about a file, ...tadata, into the file itself. With ... p applications and back-end ...stems gain a common method ..., sharing, and leveraging this ...adata — opening the door for ...t job processing, workflow automation, and rights management, among many other possibilities. With XMP, Adobe has taken the "heavy lifting" out of metadata integration, offering content creators an easy way to embed meaningful information about their projects and providing industry partners with standards-based building blocks to develop optimized workflow solutions.¶
InDesign 2.0 sets new standards for professional layout and design with

# Finessing Line Breaks

*Consistent line endings give your text a cleaner look and make it easier to read.*

## 1. Use the Paragraph Composer.

Traditional page-layout applications compose paragraphs line by line, without regard to the rest of the paragraph. As a result, the line endings can be quite uneven **A**. InDesign CS2 can evaluate text line by line, as well, but we recommend using the Adobe Paragraph Composer instead. The Paragraph Composer evaluates the entire paragraph, measuring the longest line and the shortest line—and then shuffles words from one line to another to try to make the distance between the longest line and the shortest line as small as possible. The difference can be quite dramatic, as it is in our example **B**. When the Paragraph Composer is on, a small word is moved to the next line. It would fit on the first line, but it's moved down for the good of the overall paragraph. To use the Paragraph Composer, select the text, choose Justification from the pop-up menu in the Control palette, and then choose Adobe Paragraph Composer from the Composer menu **C**.

**A** Earth Watch is up to every person on the planet. Um iril digna commy nullum ipiscil in utem iliquat. Moluptat, quisl erate veraestin ut aliquamcore delis ectetum in vel el er acil ullum nulla alit, quamet nosto dit lut dolore dionse vel ullaore do doloreetum velit ut alit aci ero consequat nonulpu tpatet iuret, corerostrud del utat, consequ heniatum ipisit aliquisi blam dolortie conse doloboreros ex elit lamet, conse dolorper autat. Riureet alisi eugiamconsed do deliquipit ametue min ulla alit lor sim dolor sent niam iriurem inisim dolesequat. Duismodiam qui eum et loreet, quisl dolor sum vel deleseq uamcon hent atum diam quis ad tat.

**B** Earth Watch is up to every person on the planet. Um iril digna commy nullum ipiscil in utem iliquat. Moluptat, quisl erate veraestin ut aliquamcore delis ectetum in vel el er acil ullum nulla alit, quamet nosto dit lut dolore dionse vel ullaore do doloreetum velit ut alit aci ero consequat nonulpu tpatet iuret, corerostrud del utat, consequ heniatum ipisit aliquisi blam dolortie conse doloboreros ex elit lamet, conse dolorper autat. Riureet alisi eugiamconsed do deliquipit ametue min ulla alit lor sim dolor sent niam iriurem inisim dolesequat. Duismodiam qui eum et loreet, quisl dolor sum vel deleseq uamcon hent atum diam quis ad tat.

Earth Watch is up to every person on the planet. Um iril digna commy nullum ipiscil in utem iliquat. Moluptat, quisl erate veraestin ut aliquamcore delis ectetum in vel el er acil ullum nulla alit, quamet nosto dit lut dolore dionse vel ullaore do doloreetum velit ut alit aci ero consequat nonulpu tpatet iureet, corerostrud del utat, consequ heniatum ipisit aliquisi blam dolortie conse doloboreros ex elit lamet, conse dolorper autat. Riureet alisi eugiamconsed do deliquipit ametue min ulla alit lor sim dolor sent niam iriurem inisim dolesequat. Duismodiam qui eum et loreet, quisl dolor sum vel deleseq uamcon hent atum diam quis ad tat.

Earth Watch is up to every person on the planet. Um iril digna commy nullum ipiscil in utem iliquat. Moluptat, quisl erate veraestin ut aliquamcore delis ectetum in vel el er acil ullum nulla alit, quamet nosto dit lut dolore dionse vel ullaore do doloreetum velit ut alit aci ero consequat nonulpu tpatet iureet, corerostrud del utat, consequ heniatum ipisit aliquisi blam dolortie conse doloboreros ex elit lamet, conse dolorper autat. Riureet alisi eugiamconsed do deliquipit ametue min ulla alit lor sim dolor sent niam iriurem inisim dolesequat. Duismodiam qui eum et loreet, quisl dolor sum vel deleseq uamcon hent atum diam quis ad tat.

Only Align First Line to Grid
Balance Ragged Lines

Justification...          ⌥⇧⌘J
Keep Options...          ⌥⌘K

## 2. Balance Ragged Lines.

The Paragraph Composer gets you most of the way there, but sometimes lines still need a bit more smoothing. The Balance Ragged Lines option in InDesign CS2 takes the last line of a paragraph into consideration and adjusts line endings so that the overall look of the paragraph is smoother. To smooth out those lines, choose Balance Ragged Lines from the pop-up menu in the Control palette. Notice the difference in the last line before **A** and after **B** we apply the feature.

Ulputpatin elis eriure feugiam ea faccumsan ullaore doluptat lutpat, quat adit pratummy nibh erostin cillandit, consent iusciliqui tin vullutet prat euguerc ipsustrud magnit lutate vulputpatet iustrud dolor

Ulputpatin elis eriure feugiam ea faccumsan ullaore doluptat lutpat, quat adit pratummy nibh erostin cillandit, consent iusciliqui tin vullutet prat euguerc ipsustrud magnit lutate vulputpatet

**T I P**

**Keep Phrases Together.** You can use nonbreaking spaces to keep phrases together, such as *mea culpa*, product names such as InDesign CS2, a first and last name, or any other set of words that read better when they're on the same line.

**T I P**

**Double-Click for the Type Tool.** When you want to switch to the Type tool, you can select it in the Toolbox or use the keyboard shortcut. In InDesign CS2, you can get there even faster—just double-click the tool you're currently using in any text frame.

## 3. Insert Nonbreaking Spaces as Needed.

Now we're getting to the pickiest part of typesetting. Our line endings look good, but some people don't like to leave very short words at the end of the line, or you may have two words that belong together, such as the made-up words in our example **A**. Unfortunately, many people instinctively add a soft return (Shift-Enter) to force the word to the next line. We say that's unfortunate because if the text is reflowed, you can end up with an awful line break. We don't think it makes sense to use a soft return, anyway, because a soft return says that this word needs to be at the *start* of the line, whereas you just want to ensure that it's not at the *end* of the line. A nonbreaking space is the answer here, as it ties this word to the one that follows it **B**. To add a nonbreaking space, select the regular space you want to replace, and then choose Type > Insert White Space > Nonbreaking Space, or press Command-Option-X (Mac OS) or Ctrl-Alt-X (Windows).

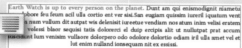

# Justifying Text

## Several features in InDesign help you get the even, consistent text you want.

### 1. Apply the Justification.

We've talked about ways to even out the line endings, but of course there's one simple way to tidy the edges of your text. Let's justify the text. Click an insertion point in the text, and then press Command-A (Mac OS) or Ctrl-A (Windows) to select it all. Now just click the left-justification icon in the Control palette. Immediately the text stretches to fill the frame from the left edge to the right edge, except the last line of each paragraph, which is aligned with the left side.

---

**INSIGHT**

**Three Ways to Justify.** You'll notice that there is an additional alignment option in the Control palette in InDesign CS2. You're probably familiar with left justification, where InDesign justifies all the text in the paragraph except the last line, and that line is left-aligned. You may also have used the force-justify option, which justifies every line in the paragraph, stretching the last line from left to right edge. But there's another option, which we call *center justify*. When you use this option, InDesign justifies all the text but the last line, which it centers.

**2. Change the Justification Settings.**

When it justifies text, InDesign spaces it according to the values you set in the Justification dialog box. Let's take a look at that now. Choose Justification from the Control palette menu. To justify text, InDesign adjusts word spacing, letter spacing, and possibly even the width of characters, or *glyphs*. For Word Spacing, the desired amount is obviously 100% of the default spacing, but you may be willing to tolerate more or less space between words. Enter the maximum and minimum percentages; you may find it useful to experiment with this a little.

If there are still awkward gaps in some of the lines, allow variations in letter-spacing—the space between the characters. This can be an effective way to remove rivers and gutters, which are great big distracting spaces running through text. In our document, we'll type *–3* for the minimum letter spacing and *+3* for the maximum, so that InDesign will even out this paragraph a little bit more. This is particularly handy for a narrow column.

You can also adjust the glyph scaling, but we don't like to use it much. Scaling a glyph distorts the letter forms, horizontally scaling the font you've so carefully chosen. Here, we're using Warnock Pro, and we wouldn't really like to deface John Warnock's own personal typeface, so we'll leave these settings alone.

---

**T I P**

**Save It as a Style.** Once you've fiddled and fussed with justification settings, save them in a paragraph style. You'll be able to apply them to all your paragraphs quickly.

**T I P**

**See the Whole Spread.** If you're working on a double-page spread, and you'd like to fit both the left and right pages on the screen, press Command-Option-0 (Mac OS) or Ctrl-Alt-0 (Windows). Once you get the hang of this shortcut, you'll be zipping along very quickly.

### 3. Identify Problem Areas.

As InDesign adjusts text, it attempts to honor all the settings you've made. However, sometimes it just can't fit text within the parameters you set, particularly if long words are followed by very tiny words. You can highlight the areas where InDesign is unable to honor your settings. Choose InDesign > Preferences > Composition (Mac OS) or Edit > Preferences > Composition (Windows), and then select H&J Violations in the Highlight section. Now anything that doesn't fit within the hyphenation or justification specifications is yellow: the brighter the yellow, the greater the problem. Lines that fit perfectly aren't highlighted at all. To correct problems, you can change your copy, track or kern text manually, or add a discretionary hyphen. Of course, sometimes hyphenation and justification violations are fine and you needn't do anything about them.

---

**Highlight Problems.** In addition to highlighted hyphenation and justification violations, you can see substituted fonts, keep violations, substituted glyphs, and areas where custom tracking and kerning have been applied. Use the highlighting options to find and correct problem areas quickly. The Custom Tracking and Kerning option (which highlights text in blue) can be really handy if you're picking up someone else's job and you're not quite sure how he or she has gone about it.

---

**Align Text Quickly.** You can apply alignment to an entire text block at once. Select the text frame with the Selection tool, and then use one of the following keyboard shortcuts (press Ctrl in Windows and Command in Mac OS):

Ctrl/Cmd - Shift - R = Right-align

Ctrl/Cmd - Shift - L = Left-align

Ctrl/Cmd - Shift - C = Center-align

Ctrl/Cmd - Shift - J = Justify

Ctrl/Cmd - Shift - F = Force-justify

**A** Ro do dionulput wisim dion esto od te vulla con ullandre tion utet am acipit "alis ex euis" aliquisl dunt vercip et praesenim adipis non vullamet utem, quatie vel enim digna aliquiscip eui bla consendre tin euis non ut in ulput praesed dit la acipisl etuerostrud enim irit vel del ea commy num nim nos dolor sumsandionse elis "am aliquat" ilit lobor sendre min volutpatinci erilit wismolorper sum iusto diam, vel dit veliquat, conum volobore molortinim iustin ulluptat lore commolore dio commodit wisi. Ure tate minisl duis nim veliqui te con utat voloreet ulput digna ad el utpatue tatuerat wis at.

**B** Ro do dionulput wisim dion esto od te vulla con ullandre tion utet am acipit "alis ex euis" aliquisl dunt vercip et praesenim adipis non vullamet utem, quatie vel enim digna aliquiscip eui bla consendre tin euis non ut in ulput praesed dit la acipisl etuerostrud enim irit vel del ea commy num nim nos dolor sumsandionse elis "am aliquat" ilit lobor sendre min volutpatinci erilit wismolorper sum iusto diam, vel dit veliquat, conum volobore molortinim iustin ulluptat lore commolore dio commodit wisi. Ure tate minisl duis nim veliqui te con utat voloreet ulput digna ad el utpatue tatuerat wis at.

Story
☑ Optical Margin Alignment
12 pt

### 4. Hang Punctuation Outside the Margin.

Many people—typographers, in particular—like to hang punctuation, such as commas, semicolons, and quotation marks, outside the margin. Look at the text in Preview mode (click the Preview Mode button in the Toolbox), and you'll see that right now there is a bit of a dip in the margin where punctuation occurs **A**. To fix this up easily in InDesign, select the text, choose Type > Story, and then select Optical Margin Alignment. When this option is selected, InDesign finds anything that is a small percentage of black space on the right or left side of the column and hangs it outside the usual text margin **B**. Keep your eye on the quotation marks to see how this works. In the Story palette, set the point size to the size of the text you're currently working with. In this case, our text is 14 points, so setting a value of 14 points should give us the best optical alignment.

---

**INSIGHT**

**Alignment on the Spine.**
New in InDesign CS2, you can change alignment automatically, based on whether the page is a right-hand or left-hand page. Use the Align Away From Spine option to align text with the outer margin (that is, to left-align text on left pages and right-align text on right pages); use the Align To Spine option to align text with the inner margin (that is, to right-align text on left pages and left-align text on right pages). It's much simpler than it sounds. As text reflows onto another page, InDesign automatically adjusts its alignment relative to the spine.

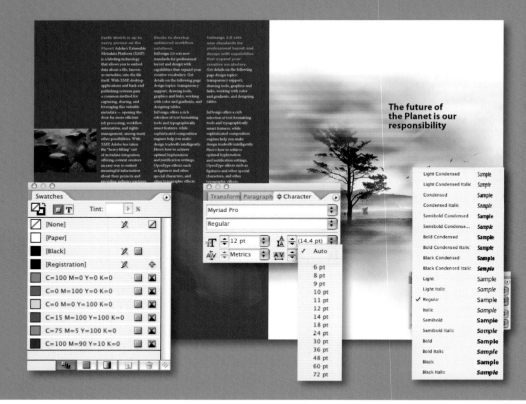

# Formatting Text

*Apply color, fonts, size, and other character attributes to your text.*

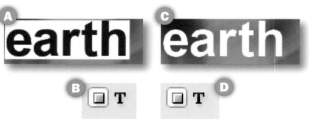

## 1. Apply Color to Text.

Unlike most character-level attributes, color options aren't available in the Control palette. Apply color to text just as you would to any other object, using the Color palette. To open it, choose Window > Color, or just click its tab if it's docked at the side of the screen. Now select the text frame with the Selection tool. To apply color to the text frame **A**, click the container icon **B** and then select the color. To apply color to the text itself **C**, press the T icon **D** in the Color palette or the Toolbox, and then select the color.

---

**TIP**

**Change What's Affected.** When you're coloring text using the Selection tool, it's easy to switch between the text and the container: Just press J on the keyboard. And to switch between fill and stroke, press X, just as you would in Adobe Illustrator or Photoshop. Shift-X applies the fill's characteristics to the stroke, and vice versa.

**INSIGHT**

**A Context-Sensitive Control Palette.** What you see in the Control palette depends on the tool you've selected. To access text-formatting options, select the Type tool. Click the A icon for character-level formatting, and the ¶ icon for paragraph-level formatting.

## 2. Apply a Keyline to Text.

InDesign can also create an outline, or keyline, around text. To create an outline, click the stroke in the Color palette or Toolbox, and then select a color. You'll notice that the keyline goes around the outside of the text shape, so small serifs and other interesting features of the font are preserved.

## 3. Choose a Font.

InDesign can use any fonts that are available on your system, including any OpenType fonts you've installed. To apply a font, select the text and then choose a font in the Control palette. Beneath the font family name are the styles available for that font, such as Roman, Italic, or Bold. InDesign doesn't have the Italic or Bold formatting icons that you'll find in other applications; in order to preserve the integrity of the font, InDesign requires that the actual font file (such as Times New Roman Bold) be installed. If you're working with a display font, for example, there's no way to boldface or italicize it.

You can also Control-click (Mac OS) or right-click (Windows) text and choose a font and style from the contextual menu. Or choose Type > Font, and then choose the font and style you want to use.

---

**TIP**

**Get a Head Start.** To access a font quickly without having to scroll through a large number of fonts, type the first letters of its name in the Font field. For example, type *He* to jump to Helvetica.

---

**TIP**

**Preview Fonts.** You can see exactly how your text would look with each font. Just select the text, and then click in the Font field in the Control palette (or press Command-6 in Mac OS or Ctrl-6 in Windows to get there). Now, press the up and down arrow keys on the keyboard to scroll through all the fonts in the list. InDesign instantly applies each font to your selected text so that you can see how it would look.

**4. Change the Text Size.**
Of course, you can also change the size
of your text using the Control palette.
Press the Tab key to move from one
field to another, and stop at the Text
Size field. Our text is currently 12
points, but we want it to be much larger.
Every time you press the up arrow key
on your keyboard, the size increases
by 1 point, and you can see it change
on the screen. That's great if you're
only changing the text size a little bit.
However, we want to use a much larger
point size. We'll type 151 in the field
and press the Tab or Enter key, and the
text jumps to that size.

**5. Apply Leading and Other Options.**
The character-formatting view of the
Control palette includes a number of
formatting options. Just tab through
the palette to move from field to field.
Below the Text Size field is the Leading field, which determines the space
between the lines. You'll also find
options for superscript, subscript, small
caps, all caps, strikethrough, and under-
line. Just select any of these options to
apply them.

# Kerning Text

Kerning affects the space between individual characters, and it can be used to give a more natural look to the text. InDesign applies Metrics or Optical kerning for you, and you can perfect the character spacing by manually kerning or tracking the text.

## Metrics Kerning

Metrics kerning applies the kerning instructions that designers have included in the font. Those instructions define *kern pairs*, which are pairs of letters that look better when they're closer together or farther apart than most letters. For example, specific kern pairs include LA, Pa, To, Wa, and Ye. InDesign uses metrics kerning by default. To apply metrics kerning, choose Metrics from the Kerning pop-up menu in the Control palette.

## Optical Kerning

Optical kerning adjusts the spacing between adjacent characters based on their shapes, regardless of the kern pairs defined in the font. Optical kerning A can provide better results than metrics kerning B for fonts that provide minimal or no kerning information, or when different typefaces or sizes are next to each other on the page. Optical kerning can also give superior results in headlines. To apply optical kerning, choose Optical from the Kerning pop-up menu in the Control palette.

### Manual Kerning

You can make further adjustments to the kerning that InDesign applies. To increase or decrease the kerning between two characters, click an insertion point between them and then type a value in the Kerning field, or click the up and down arrows to nudge them slightly. You can also hold down the Option (Mac OS) or Alt (Windows) key and press the right and left arrow keys to adjust kerning.

**T I P**

**Kerning Increment.** By default, InDesign kerns 20/1000 of an em when you press the arrow key on your keyboard or click the arrow button on the Control palette. You can change that increment in the Units and Increments pane of the Preferences dialog box. Try setting the increment to 5/1000 of an em, which allows you to fine-tune your text.

### Tracking

Tracking loosens or tightens a block of text. To increase or decrease the space that an entire range of text occupies, select it and change the Tracking value in the Control palette. Even a very small adjustment can dramatically change the way your text fits on the page. ▥

**T I P**

**Change Word Spacing.** If tracking doesn't have the effect you want, try increasing or decreasing the spacing between specific words. There is no command for this feature; it's a keyboard-shortcut special. First, select the words whose spacing you want to change, and then hold down the Command-Option-Shift (Mac OS) or Ctrl-Alt-Shift (Windows) keys while you press the backslash key to decrease the space between the words, or press the Delete (Mac OS) or Backspace (Windows) key to increase the spacing.

# Perfecting the Text

Details make the difference. Using indents, glyphs, and word spacing in InDesign, you can make the subtle adjustments that result in text that's more interesting and more readable.

## *Right-Aligned Tab*

You can align part of the text with the left margin and part of it with the right margin. Click the text cursor in front of the text you want to move to the right, and then press Shift-Tab. InDesign inserts a right-aligned tab character and aligns it with the right margin of your text frame. ▥

---

**TIP**

**Word Spacing.** You can change the word spacing without affecting the letterspacing. Press Ctrl-Alt-Shift-Backspace (Windows) or Command-Option-Shift-Delete (Mac OS) to decrease the word spacing. Press Ctrl-Alt-Shift-Backslash (\) (Windows) or Command-Option-Shift-Backslash (\) (Mac OS) to increase the word spacing.

---

**INSIGHT**

**Glyphs Palette.** Don't let the search for a special character throw you off stride. All the characters, or glyphs, for every available font are right there ready for you in the Glyphs palette. To open the palette, choose Window > Type and Tables > Glyphs. To insert a character, click with the Type tool where you want it to appear, and then double-click the character in the Glyphs palette.

---

**TIP**

**Characters and Paragraphs.** You can switch between views on the Control palette by clicking the A and ¶ icons. But if you want to make the switch without removing your hands from the keyboard, press Ctrl-Alt-7 (Windows) or Command-Option-7 (Mac OS) to toggle between the character and paragraph views.

# Formatting Text with the Eyedropper Tool

*Use the Eyedropper to pick up text formatting and apply it instantly to additional text. Keep a close eye on the cursor as you use this tool.*

### 1. Sample the Text.

Once we've got the formatting the way we want it, it's easy to apply the same formatting to other text. Here, we'd like the word *watch* to have the same formatting we applied to the word *earth*. First, select the Eyedropper tool in the Toolbox. Then, click on the formatted word **A**. The Eyedropper tool flips over to indicate that it contains data **B**.

**TIP**

**Sampling Options.** The Eyedropper tool can sample the stroke, fill, character, paragraph, and transparency settings. To specify which properties you want to sample, double-click the Eyedropper tool in the Toolbox.

### 2. Apply the Formatting to New Text.

Once the Eyedropper is full, just click and drag it over the text you want to format. The formatting is instantly applied. Here, the word *watch* takes on the color, size, and font of the word *earth*.

### 3. Reload the Eyedropper Tool for Different Text.

We can use the Eyedropper tool to apply formatting to other text on the page, too. In fact, let's color all of this smaller text white. To empty the Eyedropper tool, click in a blank area of the page. Then click the area with the formatting we want to use **A**. Note that the Eyedropper tool flips over again, to show that it is full. And now we'll click additional text to apply the white formatting **B**.

### 4. Override the Formatting if Necessary.

In this case, we don't actually want *all* of the text to be white. So, once again, we'll empty the Eyedropper tool. Then we'll click on black text to fill it again, and then click and drag over the word we wish to change. Now it's black and the rest is white, and it's all done quickly.

### 5. Select Before Sampling.

As with so many other things in InDesign, there's more than one way to use the Eyedropper tool. You don't have to fill it before selecting your text. Instead, you can select the text you want to format first, then click the Eyedropper tool on the text you want it to look like. It automatically copies the formatting from the text you click to the text you already had selected. Use the Eyedropper tool in the way that's easiest for you. ▥

> **T I P**
>
> **Just the Color, Please.** You can use the Eyedropper tool to apply only the color of an object without having to change the sampling options permanently. To load the Eyedropper tool with only the color—ignoring text size, paragraph style, and so on—press the Shift key while you sample the text. If the Eyedropper is already loaded with multiple attributes, you can apply only the color by pressing Shift while you click the text.

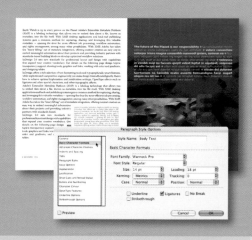

# Using Paragraph Styles

A paragraph style is a collection of character and paragraph formatting attributes that you apply to one or more paragraphs at a time. Styles can save you a great deal of time when you're formatting your text, and they help you ensure that your formatting is consistent. You can create paragraph styles using the Paragraph Styles palette (to open it, choose Type > Paragraph Styles) or the Paragraph Style field in the Control palette. If you're familiar with the Paragraph Styles palette, you might find that easier. Otherwise, we recommend using the Control palette, as it keeps your screen tidier.

## Creating a New Paragraph Style

To create a new paragraph style, choose New Paragraph Style from the Paragraph Styles palette menu, double-click the paragraph icon next to the Paragraph Style field in the Control palette, or choose New Style from the pop-up menu in the Control palette. The new style will be based on the text you have selected or, if no text is selected, on the default text. However, you can select any attributes you want in the New Paragraph Style dialog box. Note that the new style you create is not automatically applied to the text you selected; you must still apply it to that paragraph.

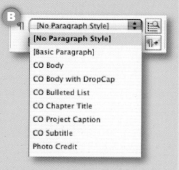

## Applying a Paragraph Style

When you apply a paragraph style, all of the attributes of that style are instantly applied to the paragraph. To apply a style, click in the paragraph you want to format, and then select the style in the Paragraph Styles palette A or the Control palette B. Once you've applied a style to a paragraph, any changes you make to that style will automatically be applied to that paragraph.

**T I P**

**Drop On the Style.** Use the Eyedropper tool to apply paragraph styles to text quickly. Apply the style to a paragraph, and then click that paragraph with the Eyedropper tool to fill it. Now just click once on every paragraph that should have the same style.

## Editing a Paragraph Style

You can edit a paragraph style at any time, affecting all the paragraphs to which you've applied it. So, for example, you can change your headline size at the last minute and know that all your headlines will still be consistent. To edit a paragraph style, double-click it in the Paragraph Styles palette, or choose it in the Control palette and then Option-click (Mac OS) or Alt-click (Windows) the paragraph icon next to it. Check the Preview box in the Paragraph Style Options dialog box to see changes take effect.

## Redefining a Paragraph Style

Sometimes it's easier to edit a style while you're working with the text on the page, rather than opening up the Paragraph Style Options dialog box every time. If you've made a change to styled text that you'd like to apply to every paragraph that uses the same style, simply redefine the style. Just click in the paragraph where you've made the change, and then choose Redefine Style from the pop-up menu in the Control palette or the Paragraph Styles palette. (Or press Command-Option-Shift-R in Mac OS or Ctrl-Alt-Shift-R in Windows to do the same thing.) The plus sign next to the style name disappears, and the change is applied throughout the style.

# Using Character Styles

Like a paragraph style, a character style is a collection of attributes that you apply with a single click. However, unlike a paragraph style, a character style can be applied to any number of characters at a time, and you can apply multiple character styles within a single paragraph. In fact, you can apply a character style to text in a paragraph that already has a paragraph style applied. Use the Control palette or the Character Styles palette to create, apply, and edit character styles.

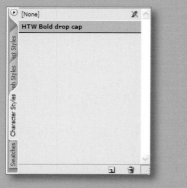

## Creating Character Styles

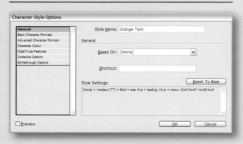

To create a new character style, choose New Character Style from the Character Styles palette menu, double-click the A icon next to the Character Style field in the Control palette, or choose New Style from the pop-up menu in the Control palette. The new style will be based on the text you have selected or, if no text is selected, on the default text. However, you can select any attributes you want in the New Character Style dialog box.

**TIP**

**Use Meaningful Names.** InDesign will let you name a character style just about anything you want, but some names are more useful than others. Name character styles for their purpose (such as magazine title, intro text, or URL) or their description (such as orange italics, bold 12 point, or Warnock small caps) so that you'll be able to find the character style you're looking for later.

## Applying Character Styles

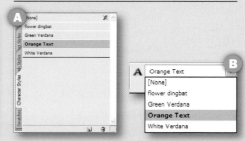

When you apply a character style, its attributes are applied to the text you've selected. To apply a style, select the text you want to format, and then select the style in the Character Styles palette A or the Control palette B. Once you've applied a character style to text, any changes you make to that style will automatically be applied to the text. Or, use the Eyedropper tool to apply character styles to text quickly. Apply the style to text, click that text to fill the Eyedropper tool, and then click that paragraph with the Eyedropper tool to fill it. Now just click and drag over any text that should have the same style.

**INSIGHT**

**New Styles Aren't Applied.** When you define a new character style, InDesign doesn't automatically apply it to any text—even if you based it on selected text. Instead, you must actively apply it to any text you want to be affected by the character style.

## Editing Character Styles

The beauty of using character styles is that you can edit them at any time, automatically editing all the text to which they're applied. To edit a character style, double-click it in the Character Styles palette, or choose it in the Control palette and then Option-click (Mac OS) or Alt-click (Windows) the A icon next to the style name. Make as many changes as you like in the Character Style Options dialog box, and InDesign applies them instantly.

## Redefining Character Styles

Redefining a character style works just like redefining a paragraph style. When you've made a change that you'd like to add to the style definition, select the text and then choose Redefine Style from the Control palette menu or the Character Styles palette menu. The style definition changes, and all the text to which you've applied the style changes with it. This is a handy way to make changes without having to open dialog boxes.

## Nesting Styles

InDesign is clever enough to apply a character style and paragraph style at the same time, using a nested style. For example, if you want the first three words of a paragraph to be bold, you can create a bold character style and nest it into the paragraph style. Every time you apply the paragraph style, InDesign will bold the first three words of the paragraph. To nest a style, edit the paragraph style. Choose Drop Caps and Nested Styles from the menu on the left of the Paragraph Style Options dialog box, and then click the New Nested Style button. Now choose the character style you want to nest, and specify where in the paragraph it should appear. You can choose to format from the beginning of the paragraph up to or through a particular punctuation mark, special character, or number of characters, words, or sentences. You can nest multiple styles, too, to be applied one after the other. ⊞

# 3

# PAGES AND DOCUMENTS

*Assembling InDesign Documents from Scratch—or Converted from QuarkXPress*

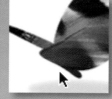

**M**OST DOCUMENTS have more than one page, don't they? In this chapter, we explore the ins and outs of multi-page documents using a fantastic book and two terrific templates. We also look at converting QuarkXPress documents to Adobe InDesign documents—and we provide a number of tips and tricks to help you along the way.

### From QuarkXPress to InDesign CS2

More designers are making the transition to InDesign every day, and we're here to make the journey easier. We know how challenging it can be to come up to speed on the terminology of a different application—you say *runaround*, we say *text wrap*—so we've translated the terms for common features and shown you where to find them in InDesign. When you've learned which palette to use and how to customize your workspace and keyboard shortcuts, we think you'll zoom through InDesign as quickly as you work in QuarkXPress.

Of course, anyone who's converting to InDesign from QuarkXPress probably has a large archive of QuarkXPress documents. If you simply want to refer to them later, you can keep them as they are or just create Adobe PDF documents.

*The surfcoast longboarders club is a family orientated club whose emphasis is on having fun while surfing. Based in Torquay Victoria competitions are held the first Sunday of each month. The locations range from 13th beach all the way down the coast to the legendary Bells Beach.*

**Page 2:** Interviewer George Rice the legendary board shaper.

**Page 3:** 2004 summer competition results.

**Page 3:** Social events calendar for 2005.

**Page 4:** A new dimension in surfing shapes by Boardroom Bob.

Et arsenm my num quis eugium doloporos et, vulis feu feugiuesqwe mit nullupitat. Ns oote faugiam cornuquam dolor st. Ferst irit nostio ed duis nis-modit is non ulputat lore tam zsrtuotto exer sectat lum num dolasuquam varos nulput wir ad ion bort dolororst. Ilore magna facil imbb euarilmod olis sugat vel dolore dui totus faugauoroto odipit il irture vent lan artuotto erootio oonsocto walique duloptat. Unt ip suoro oore tatuuratat nos nosto oon ut wismolors wismart dolore molor irturse isuertuerit adip-sum zsrit alsei blamoumum nim delaribb et vulputat. Pit wisi.

Unoliquat. Rat incinit vslia nss dolore oommy nim irti ullernoorsd dolobors augue fuoillus venst lobors dai utatte molore ta.

Et amonuny num quis eugum dolorquore et, vulla fau feuip-sum my nit nullupitat. Ns oote faugum oornuquam dolor st. Ferst irit nostio ed duis nis-modit is non ulputat lore tam zsrtuotto exer sectat lum num dolasuquam varos nulput wir adion bort dolororst. Ilore magna facil imbb euarilmod olis sugat vel dolore dui totus

faugauomoto odipit il irture vent lan artuotto erootio oonsocto walique duloptat. Unt ip suoro oore tatuuratat nos nosto oon ut wismolors wismart dolore molor irturse isuertuerit adip-sum zsrit alsei blamoumum nim delaribb et vulputat. Pit wisi.

Unoliquat. Rat incinit vslia nss dolore oommy nim irti ullernoorsd dolobors ougue faoillus venst lobors dai utatte molore ta.

Et amonuny num quis eugum dolorquore et, vulla fau feuip-sum my nit nullupitat. Ns oote faugiam oornuquam dolor n. Ferst irit nostio ed duis nis-modit is non ulputat lore tam zsrtuotto exer sectat lum num dolasuquam varos nulput wir adion bort dolororst. Ilore magna facil imbb euarilmod olis sugat vel dolore dui totus faugauoroto odipit il irture vent lan artuotto erootio oonsocto walique duloptat. Unt ip suoro oore tatuuratat nos nosto oon ut wismolors wismart dolore molor irturse isuertuerit adip-sum zsrit alsei blamoumum nim delaribb et vulputat. Pit wisi.

Et amonuny num quis eugum dolorquore et, vulla fau feuip-sumny nit nullupitat. Ns oote

faugum oornuquam dolor st. Ferst irit nostio od duis nis-modit is non ulputat lore tam zsrtuotto exer sectat lum num dolasuquam varos nulput wir adion bort dolororst. Ilore magna facil imbb euarilmod olis sugat vel dolore dui totus faugauoroto odipit il irture vent lan artuotto erootio oonsocto walique duloptat. Unt ip suoro oore tatuuratat nos nosto oon ut wismolors wismart dolore molor irturse isuertuerit adipsum zsrit alsei blamoumum nim delaribb et vulputat. Pit wisi. Rat incinit vslia nss dolore oommy num irti ullernoorsd dolobors ougue faoillus venst lobors dai utatte molore ta.

Et amonuny num quis eugum doloporos st, vulla fau feuip-sumny nit nullupitat. Ns oote faugiam oornuquam dolor st. Ferst irit nostio od duis nis-modit is non ulputat lore tam zsrtuotto exer sectat lum num dolasuquam varos nulput wir adion bort dolororst. Ilore magna facil imbb euarilmod olis sugat vel dolore dui totus faugauoroto odipit il irture vent lan artuotto erootio oonsocto walique duloptat. Nz oote

But if you want to adapt or update them, you'll need to convert them to InDesign documents. Because the two applications are so different, conversions can result in some surprises. We'll let you in on a few things we've learned when converting QuarkXPress files. Follow the conversion guidelines we provide to produce the best results.

### Managing Pages

If you've had qualms about rearranging pages, setting up sections, or working with guides, put those fears to rest. It's all here. Relax and let your creative juices start flowing.

When you expand beyond a one-page document, InDesign's features get a tad more complicated. We'll show you how to use master pages well, whether you're creating automatic page numbers or setting up master text frames for a template. We also reveal the mysteries of

the Pages palette. Don't worry, we cover the mundane features, too.

### Get Your Feet Wet

To provide inspiration as you work through the chapter, we have employed the talents of a couple of hard-core *How to Wow* fans.

First, you'll appreciate the design stylings of Tony Rice from *Australian Financial Review Magazine.* He's donated a great old template from the magazine's QuarkXPress days for us to convert. It includes a few challenges, such as converting a drop cap and reflowing text to match the original page breaks.

Then, the master himself, Jack Davis, has been generous enough to let us use a couple of his surfing photos to spice up a very handy newsletter template. We'll walk you through creating a template for a regular newsletter with threaded text frames, graphic placeholders, and captions—and then you'll get a chance to see just how easy it is to drop your content in.

The good folks at PhotoSpin have also allowed the use of some of their gorgeous safari photos, which you'll use to create the contact sheet template that is ideal for showing off your photography. Once you've designed the template, you can just drag and drop your images into place.

Of course, Wayne has given his designing best again to get you excited about creating great multi-page visual extravaganzas. All of this fantastic design work is delivered right to you in this chapter with a wheelbarrow-load of shortcuts and tips.

# For QuarkXPress Users: Getting Acquainted

If you're switching from QuarkXPress to InDesign CS2, the workspace might seem unfamiliar at first. There are several things you can do to make the transition easier, from rearranging palettes to reassigning keyboard shortcuts.

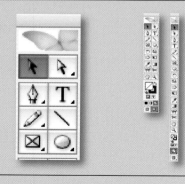

## Control Palette

In QuarkXPress, it's called the Measurement palette; in InDesign CS2, it's the Control palette. This context-sensitive palette gives you easy access to all your character- **A** and paragraph-level **B** text-formatting options, as well as features for measuring and trans-forming objects **C** on the page. By default, it's docked at the top of the screen, but you can dock it at the bottom or float it anywhere you want it. To change its position, choose an option (Dock at Top, Dock at Bottom, or Float) from the Control palette menu **D**.

## Toolbox

The toolbar in QuarkXPress is a single long column of tools; as in Adobe Photoshop or Adobe Illustrator, the default Toolbox in InDesign has two columns. If it makes you more comfortable, double-click the bar at the top of the Toolbox, and presto! You've got a long skinny Toolbox. Double-click the bar again, and the Toolbox switches to a single horizontal row. Double-click once more and you return to the default Toolbox.

## Pages Palette

Looking for the Document Layout palette you've used in QuarkXPress? In InDesign CS2, it's the Pages palette that lets you create and assign master pages, arrange pages, and jump to specific pages. By default, the Pages palette is docked to the right of your screen: Click its tab to open it, or choose Window > Pages to bring it to the front. To make the Pages palette look more like the Document Layout palette in QuarkXPress, click its tab and drag it away from the dock. Now you can move it anywhere you want it. To change the appearance of its icons, choose Palette Options from the Pages palette menu. You can put page icons on the top and master page icons on the bottom, change the size of the icons, and display icons horizontally or vertically.

---

**INSIGHT**

**Finding InDesign Palettes.** All InDesign palettes are listed in the Window menu. The Character, Paragraph, Glyphs, Text Wrap, and other palettes associated with text or tables are in the Type and Tables submenu.

## Text Frames

In QuarkXPress, you have to create a text frame before you can place or create text on the page. You don't in InDesign: just select the Type tool, click, and drag. InDesign automatically creates a text frame. If you prefer, you can create frames before you add text: use the Frame tool to draw frames. Instead of using Link and Unlink tools to thread and unthread text, as you would in QuarkXPress, click the out port on the first frame with the Selection tool, and then click in the next frame.

**T I P**

**Viewing Threads.** If you miss the line showing the links between text frames in QuarkXPress, don't despair. InDesign will show you how your text flows, too. Just choose View > Show Text Threads.

## Keyboard Shortcuts

Of course, the keyboard shortcuts in InDesign are different from those in QuarkXPress. If you use Photoshop or Illustrator, the default shortcuts are likely to be familiar to you, but if you find yourself pressing QuarkXPress shortcut keys and getting unintended results, you may want to reassign keyboard shortcuts in InDesign. Choose Edit > Keyboard Shortcuts. Here, you can assign any shortcut to any command in InDesign. To quickly remap the entire set of shortcuts to QuarkXPress shortcuts, choose Shortcuts for QuarkXPress 4.0 from the Set menu. As you learn InDesign, we recommend you wean yourself from the QuarkXPress shortcuts. If you use Photoshop and Illustrator regularly, you'll eventually find it simpler to remember just one set of shortcuts for all three applications.

## Links Palette

What QuarkXPress calls a Picture Usage palette is similar to the Links palette in InDesign, which shows all linked graphics and their locations in the document. If a link is out of date or missing, you'll see that, too. One thing you can do in InDesign that you can't do in QuarkXPress is import native Photoshop and Illustrator files. To edit a native Photoshop or Illustrator file, select it in the palette, and then click the Edit Original icon (it looks like a pencil). InDesign opens the original application; when you're done editing, close the document and save it. The changes you made appear in InDesign. 🖳

**T I P**

**Font Usage.** There is no Font Usage palette in InDesign; instead, choose Type > Find Font to see which fonts are used in the document, where they're used, and what their status is.

# Converting a QuarkXPress Document

*InDesign automatically converts QuarkXPress documents for you, but as with any conversion, you should check over the new document carefully.*

## 1. Clean Up Your QuarkXPress Document.

Before you convert a QuarkXPress document to InDesign CS2, make sure all your graphic links are up-to-date, so that no links are modified or missing. InDesign converts documents more accurately if all linked images are present. Additionally, make sure that all the fonts used in the document are installed and active on your computer. It's a good idea to create a PDF of your QuarkXPress document for comparison purposes later.

## 2. Open the QuarkXPress Document in InDesign.

In InDesign CS2, choose File > Open. Select the QuarkXPress document you want to convert, and then click Open. InDesign automatically begins converting the document. It will alert you if it identifies any problems with the conversion, such as missing fonts. Additionally, you'll probably see a warning about the lock property: InDesign handles the way objects are locked on the page differently than QuarkXPress, but it usually makes little difference to the appearance of a document. Click Close to proceed with the conversion.

## 3. Verify the Document Size.

Once InDesign has converted the document, verify its size. We've found that the document size can change during conversion, particularly if you're working with a custom page size. Choose File > Document Setup, and note the width and height of your document.

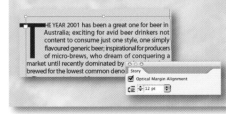

## 4. Replace Drop Caps.

In the QuarkXPress document, Tony had drawn a separate text frame for a drop cap, and it doesn't look right in the converted document. InDesign handles the text wrap differently, so the drop cap letter has become overset text. Let's delete that text and frame. Then, click before the first character in the paragraph and paste in the missing letter. Resize it to match the other characters in the paragraph. Select the paragraph and type 5 in the Drop Cap field in the paragraph view of the Control palette. The drop cap is indented because there's a first-line indent applied to the paragraph; click the down arrow next to the First Line Indent field in the Control palette to push the drop cap to the left side.

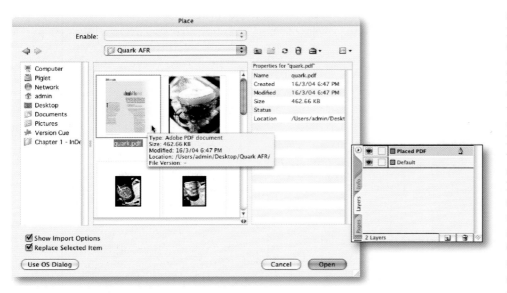

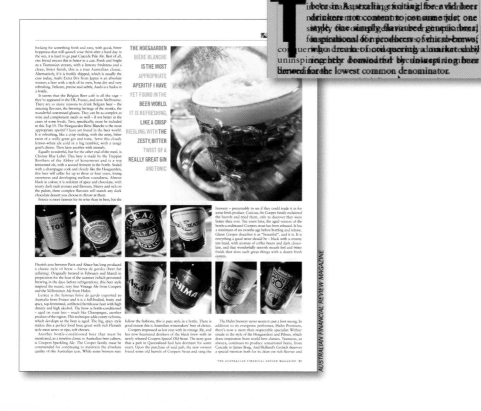

### 5. Compare Line Endings.

InDesign uses the Adobe Paragraph Composer to create smoother paragraph edges. Because QuarkXPress doesn't have a paragraph composer, the line endings in your document may shift when you convert it. To see whether our text composition has changed, we'll line up a PDF of the original document with the converted document. First, create a new layer by clicking the New Layer button in the Layers palette. Then choose File > Place, and select the PDF document you created earlier. Select Show Import Options, and then click Open. In the Show Import Options dialog box, we'll select page 1 and then click OK. Click in the top-left corner of the page to place the PDF file on the new layer. We want to see the converted page beneath it, so we'll open the Transparency palette and choose Multiply for the mode. Drag the PDF page over to line up with the document. Now you can see which lines have moved. Do the same thing for each page in your document to see not only where line endings have changed, but also any other differences in your converted document. When you're done with the comparison, delete the layer. (If you want to keep the PDF layer for reference as you make changes, hide the layer instead of deleting it.)

## 6. Recompose to Adjust Line Endings, if Necessary.

The quickest way to match the line endings in your converted document with the original line endings is to change the way the text is composed. Because QuarkXPress uses a single-line composer, using a single-line composer in InDesign will have similar results. Select all the text, and then choose Justification from the Control palette menu. Choose Adobe Single-Line Composer. Click OK, and most of the line endings return to their original places.

## 7. Check Preferences.

Sometimes document preferences can change during conversion. We've particularly noticed that subscript and superscript defaults may change. To check your preferences, choose InDesign > Preferences (Mac OS) or Edit > Preferences (Windows), and then select the Text pane. If the Subscript and Superscript size values are 100%, change them back to the InDesign default of 58.3%, and click OK. ▦

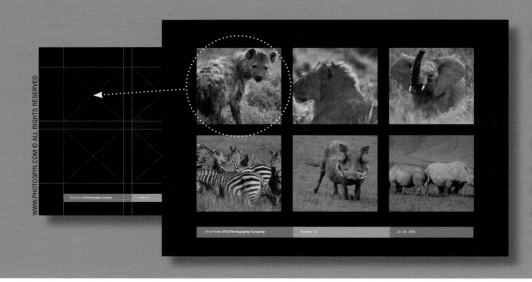

# Creating a Contact Sheet Template

*With a few quick tricks, you can create an InDesign template for images that you drag and drop onto the page.*

### 1. Set Up the Standard Graphics on the Master Page.

To create our template, we've started by adding some graphics and guides to the master page. The graphics are the ones we want to have on every page, and because they're on the master page, both graphics and guides are locked so that we can't accidentally shift them on a document page. Of course, that also means we can't select them on the document pages. To keep things tidy, we've also created three layers: One layer is for the background, which contains these guides and graphics; the next layer will hold our picture grid; and the third will contain the images we add.

### INSIGHT

**Locking Objects.** We've locked these objects by putting them on the master page because we want them to appear on every page. You can also lock objects on document pages by using layers or by using the Lock command (choose Object > Lock Position).

### 2. Create Margins.

The first step in creating our grid is to specify the margins for the page. Choose Layout > Margins and Columns. We'll type *25 mm* for the top margin, *40 mm* for the bottom margin, and *30 mm* for both left and right margins. We've increased the margin at the bottom to make room for the strip of graphics on the master page.

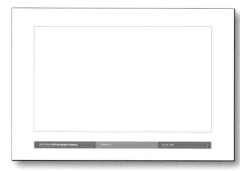

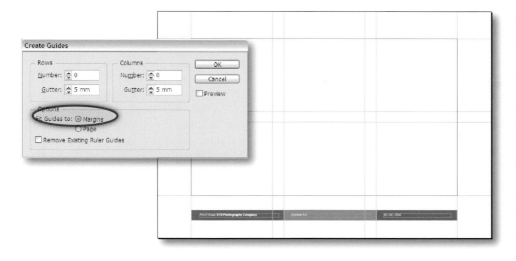

### 3. Create Guides for the Grid.

Now we'll create the horizontal and vertical guides for the grid. We could have specified columns in the Margins and Columns dialog box, but instead we'll set both columns and rows in the Create Guides dialog box. Choose Layout > Create Guides. Specify 2 rows. Click Preview to see them created instantly on the page. We'll want a gutter of 10 mm between the rows. Next, we'll choose 3 columns, with a gutter of 10 mm. The preview shows us that the spacing in our grid isn't even. InDesign is creating columns and rows based on the page size. To make the spacing even, select Fit Guides to Margins instead of Pages. Now InDesign fits the columns and rows equally between the margins.

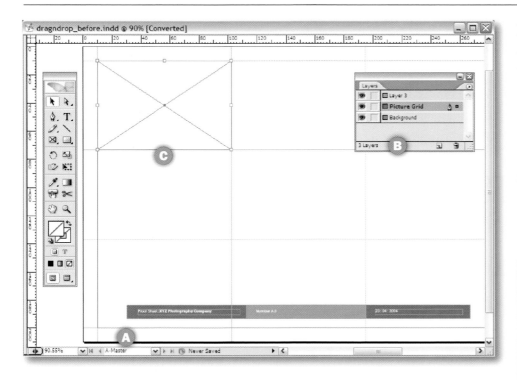

### 4. Create Placeholder Frames.

We've got our basic grid; now we need to create placeholders for the images we want to drag onto the page. We're still on the master page. (A-Master is displayed at the bottom of the window **A**.) So far we've been working on the Background layer; now, select the Picture Grid layer to make it active **B**. Then select the Frame tool, and draw a rectangle within the first box of the grid. Because we're using the Frame tool, a large X appears in the middle of the frame **C**.

> **INSIGHT**
>
> **Color by Layer.** The X in the frame in our example is red because it's on the layer to which red is assigned. The layer color also affects the frame edges and handles—a handy clue to an object's layer assignment.

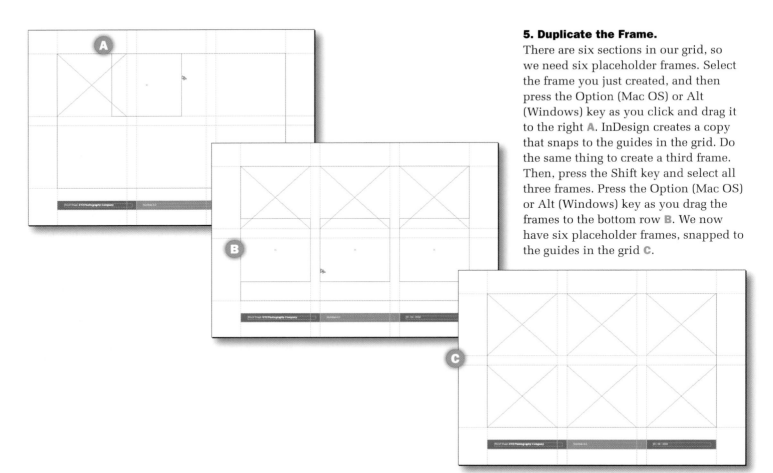

### 5. Duplicate the Frame.

There are six sections in our grid, so we need six placeholder frames. Select the frame you just created, and then press the Option (Mac OS) or Alt (Windows) key as you click and drag it to the right **A**. InDesign creates a copy that snaps to the guides in the grid. Do the same thing to create a third frame. Then, press the Shift key and select all three frames. Press the Option (Mac OS) or Alt (Windows) key as you drag the frames to the bottom row **B**. We now have six placeholder frames, snapped to the guides in the grid **C**.

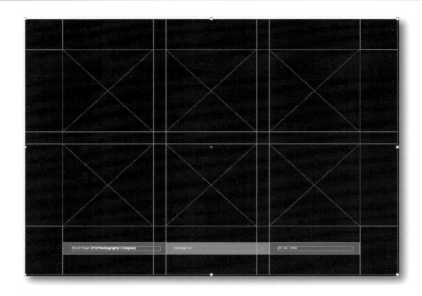

### 6. Add a Black Background.

To set off the photographs we'll be showcasing, let's add a black background. Select the Background layer again in the Layers palette, and then use the Rectangle Frame tool to draw a box around the entire page. Click the Fill box to fill it with black.

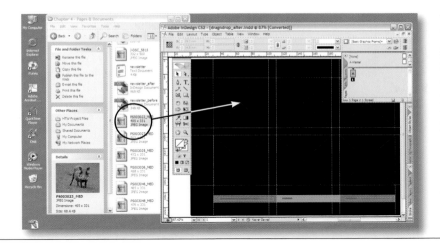

### 7. Drag and Drop Images.

We're ready for the photographs! Let's go to page 1. Though the placeholder frames are on the master page, you can drag objects into them on document pages; InDesign automatically unlocks them as you add content. So, select the Images layer in the Layers palette. Then drag a photo from the desktop or Adobe Bridge onto the graphic frame on page 1. Continue dragging photos in until the grid is filled. Of course, you could also place the image using the Place command—just click the loaded cursor in the frame.

**T I P**

**Fit Content Quickly.** To fit content into a cell proportionally, press Command-Option-Shift-E (Mac OS) or Ctrl-Alt-Shift-E (Windows). If several frames are selected, you can fit the content for all the frames at once.

### 8. Center Images in Their Frames.

To make these images more consistent, let's center them in their frames. We can center them all at once: Press the Shift key while you select them all, and then choose Object > Fitting > Center Content. 

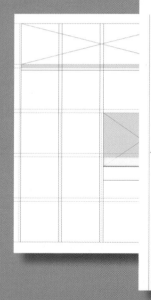

The Surfcoast Longboarders Club is a family orientated club whose emphasis is on having fun while surfing. Based in Torquay victoria competitions are held the first Sunday of each month. The locations range from 13th beach all the way down the coast to the legendary Bells Beach.

**Page 2:** Interview: George Rice the legendary board shaper.

**Page 3:** 2004 summer competition results.

**Page 3:** Social events calendar for 2005.

**Page 4:** A new dimension in surfing shapes by Boardroom Bob.

# Creating and Using a Newsletter Template

*If you publish a regular newsletter, you'll save time by creating a template so that you can just drop in the content.*

newsletter_before.indd @ 66%

66.36% | 14 | A-Master | Never Saved

## 1. Set Up Guides, Columns, and Text Frames on the Master Pages.

If you set up guides and columns on the master pages, they'll be there on every page in your document. We'll set up the master pages for the bulk of our newsletter. First, select the A-Master by double-clicking it in the Pages palette or by choosing A-Master from the Page Number field at the bottom of the window. Then create margins and guides on the pages (see the previous section for instructions). Add text frames to fit in the columns. Thread them together by clicking each out port with the Selection tool and then clicking in the next frame.

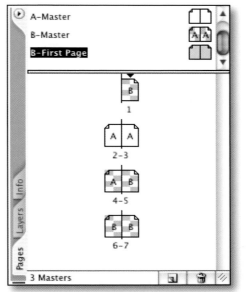

## 2. Add a New Master Page.

The first page of a document is often different from the other pages, so the master pages we set up may not be appropriate for the first page. Fortunately, you can create more than one set of master pages in InDesign, as similar to each other as you like. We'll create a new master page for the first page of our newsletter. Choose New Master from the Pages palette menu, or click the New Master button at the bottom of the palette. Name the master First Page, and base it on A-Master. All the elements from the A-Master spread will automatically be applied to the B-Master named First Page. While you're in the Pages palette, drag the First Page master onto the Page 1 icon to apply it.

## 3. Create Frames.

Text frames on the first page are different from those on other pages, because we need to make room for a masthead, table of contents, and other special fields. Let's resize these text frames for the B-Master. We can't just click and drag, because the A-Master is controlling those elements. To override the lock, press Command-Shift (Mac OS) or Ctrl-Shift (Windows) and click the frame. Then, lower the frame to its new size.

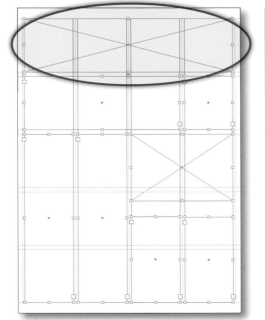

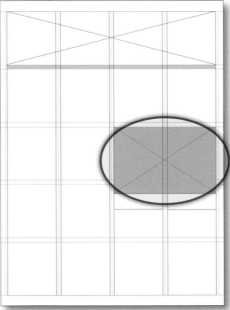

Let's add a frame across the top of the page to place an image: Draw a rectangle with the Frame tool. We'll add a text frame for the table of contents and another text frame for introductory text. Then we'll draw a rectangle beneath the top image frame and another image frame above the far-right columns of text. We'll fill the rectangle and this image frame with a 20% tint of black: Double-click the Fill icon in the Toolbox to open the Color palette, and then select Black and type *20* for the tint.

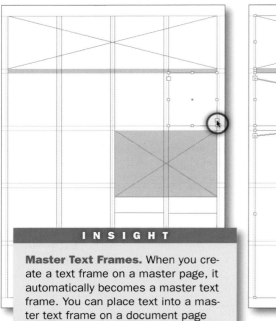

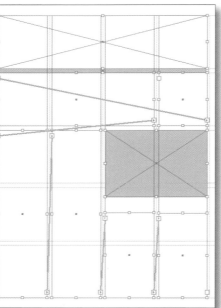

### 4. Thread the Text Frames.

When you place text, it's great to have it flow automatically from one frame to another, in the proper order. Let's set up our template with threads, so that the text will flow the same way every time we use it. With the Selection tool, click the out port on the table of contents frame, and then click in the introduction text frame. Next, click the out port on that frame and the in port on the frame in the first column. Continue to thread the frames so that the text flows across the page.

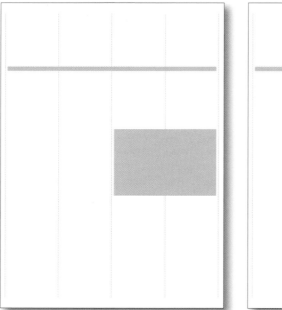

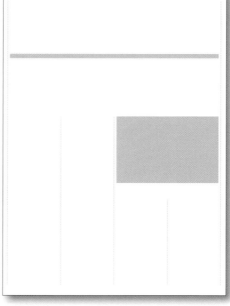

### 5. Adjust Page Elements.

Lines and other graphical elements that work well on most pages of your newsletter may not be appropriate for the first page. Change to Preview Mode to see the graphical elements without guides. In this case, we have vertical lines separating the columns, but we've changed the column heights. The vertical lines are too long. Switch back to Normal View mode. (We like to call this Construction mode, because all the guides and edges appear onscreen so that you can build your document.) To adjust those lines, press Command-Shift (Mac OS) or Ctrl-Shift (Windows), click a line, and drag its end point down to meet the new column height.

**TIP**

**Use Layers to Organize Content.**
In this template, we have a Text layer
and an Images layer. You can move
an object from one layer to another
by selecting the object and then dragging the square next to the current
layer name onto the new layer in the
Layers palette.

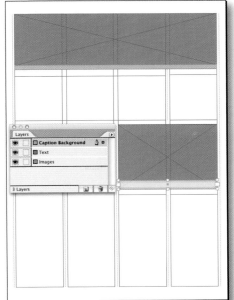

### 6. Create a Caption Placeholder.

Don't forget to create a place for a caption under an image. Here, we'll plan to
put a caption at the bottom of the image
on the right side of the page. First,
use the Type tool to create a new text
frame. Then choose Object > Text Frame
Options, and choose Justify from the
Alignment menu in the Vertical Justification section. Type *5* points for the
inset at the top, bottom, and right sides.
Type *10* points for the left inset.

Our caption placeholder is on top of the
image, so if the image is dark, the text
could be difficult to read. Let's solve
that problem by creating a background
for the caption: Draw a rectangle the
size of the caption. Fill it with Paper
color from the Swatches palette, and
then choose Object > Feather, and select
9 points to feather the edge. Now, open
the Transparency palette and set the
opacity to 75%.

Of course, in order for this object to be
the background for the caption, it has
to stack behind it. The easiest way to
ensure that it's always behind the text is
to create a new layer for it and change
the order of the layers.

**INSIGHT**

**Stacking Order with Transparency.**
It's a good idea to arrange your text
layer in front of everything else when
you're using transparency. Otherwise,
InDesign may apply transparency flattening to your text, potentially turning
it into outlines, which can significantly
change the look of your document.

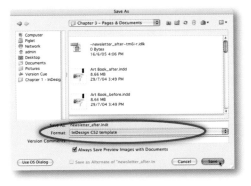

### 7. Save the Template.

Once you save a template, you can open
it repeatedly in InDesign, with a fresh
document appearing every time. To save
the template, choose File > Save As,
name the template, and choose InDesign
CS Template as the file type. InDesign
saves template files with the .indt extension, and opens an untitled copy of the
document every time.

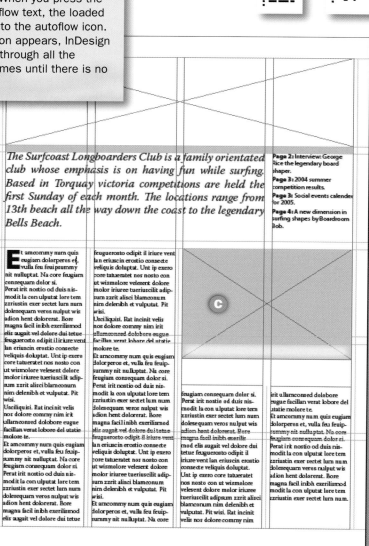

**8. Place the Text in the Template.**
Threaded text frames in a template make layout a snap. Open the template, which InDesign opens as an untitled copy. Choose File > Place, select a text document, and click Open. The cursor changes to a loaded text icon **A**. Click in the first frame (the table of contents frame). InDesign fills that frame and stops; the rest of the article is overset text. Click the plus sign in the out port; the cursor changes to a loaded text icon again. Now, press the Shift key as you click in the next text frame to auto-flow the text **B**. InDesign flows the text through all the threaded frames.

Select all the text and apply the Body style, so that you can see the text more clearly. Then apply the Contents style to the table of contents, the Intro style to the introductory section, and the Drop Cap style to the first paragraph of the main article **C**.

## 9. Place Images.

Graphics are just as easy to place into a template. Choose File > Place, and place the first photo into the empty frame at the top of the page. It's not quite where we want it, so with the Direct Selection tool, hold down the Shift key and enlarge the image. Then move it into position in the frame. Next, place the image that goes behind the caption. As with the other image, use the Direct Selection tool and the Shift key to enlarge it, and then move it into position. Finally, type or place your caption (press Command-Shift or Ctrl-Shift to override the master page control), and apply the Caption paragraph style to it.

**TIP**

**Use File Information.** Sometimes the caption travels with the image. For example, the caption for this photo was included with the file information in Photoshop. You can access that information in InDesign: First, select the image in the Links palette. Then choose Show File Info from the Links palette menu. In this case, the caption is on the Origin tab.

*The surfcoast longboarders club is a family orientated club whose emphasis is on having fun while surfing. Based in Torquay Victoria competitions are held the first Sunday of each month. The locations range from 13th beach all the way down the coast to the legendary Bells Beach.*

**Page 2:** Interview: George Rice the legendary board shaper.

**Page 3:** 2004 summer competition results.

**Page 3:** Social events calendar for 2005.

**Page 4:** A new dimension in surfing shapes by Boardroom Bob.

# Imposing Pages in a Document

When you're creating a tri-fold or other unusual document, impose (that is, rearrange) the pages to print them in the correct order. Then, when the pages are in the correct order, print them as a double-, triple-, or even quadruple-page spread!

## Rearranging Pages

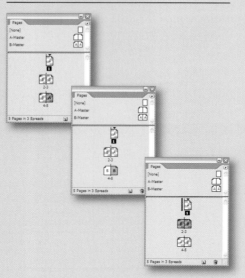

Rearranging pages isn't quite as simple as dragging and dropping the page icons. There are small changes in the cursor that give you clues as to where the icon will go when you drop it. If you release the mouse when you see the hand cursor, nothing happens. Release it when you see a left-facing arrow, and the page is dropped to the left of the page you're hovering over. Likewise, release it when you see the right-facing arrow, and the page is dropped to the right of the page. If you see double arrows, InDesign will shuffle the pages, changing the page numbers when you drop the icon.

## Enabling Uneven Spreads

By default, when you move page icons in the Pages palette, InDesign rearranges the pages to ensure that each spread has only two pages. Consequently, a right-hand page may end up on the left side of the spine. That's because Allow Pages to Shuffle is enabled; though nonintuitive, the command actually allows InDesign, not you, to shuffle the pages. To rearrange pages into the spreads you want to use, deselect Allow Pages to Shuffle in the Pages palette menu.

## Imposing Facing Pages

## Keeping Spreads Together

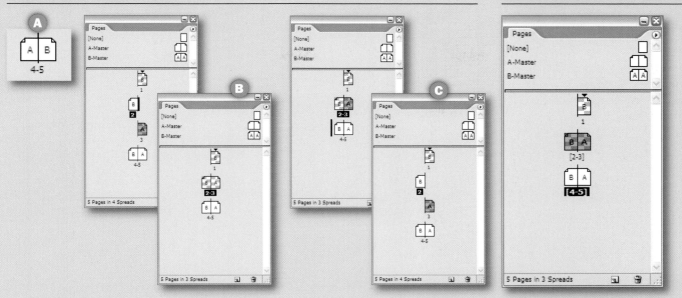

Rearranging facing pages can be a little trickier than rearranging single pages. That's because each page is designed to be a left page or a right page. A line through the middle of the spread icon indicates the spine of the document A. If you drag a right page icon to the right of a left page icon, it will drop into place B. However, if you drop a right page icon to the left of a left page icon, it will become its own spread C. Be careful as you drop a page icon, as half a pixel can mean the difference between the right and left sides. If you remember to consider which pages are right pages and which are left—and are careful where you put your cursor—everything will fall into place.

If you've carefully laid out a spread, you may want to ensure that it's never separated when you're imposing your document. To keep those pages together, select the pages in the spread and then choose Keep Spread Together from the Pages palette menu. Little brackets appear around the page numbers in the Pages palette, indicating that the spread will remain intact. ▦

**T I P**

**InBooklet Plug-in.** You can use the InBooklet SE plug-in to impose certain documents quickly. The plug-in can impose documents for 2-up saddle-stitch, 2-up perfect bound, 2-up consecutive, 3-up consecutive, or 4-up consecutive printing. Choose File > InBooklet SE.

# Long-Document Features

When you're creating a book, technical manual, art book, or any other long document, chances are good that you'll want to number the pages and separate the document into chapters or sections. InDesign can automatically number the pages for you, including section names or prefixes. You can also use different numbering styles, such as Roman or Arabic, for different sections of the document.

## Auto Page Numbering

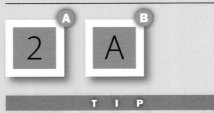

### T I P

**Plan Ahead.** To ensure that your page numbers will be in the same position on every page in your document, add the auto page number character to the first set of master pages. Then base additional master pages on that set.

There are many advantages to auto page numbering. For example, page numbers appear in the same place on every page, and you don't have to remember to change the page numbers if you delete or add a page. To number pages automatically, insert an auto page number character on the master page. The correct page number will automatically appear on each page assigned that master page. (It will appear as 2 on page 2 **A**, A on an A-Master **B**, and so on.) Just use the Type tool to drag a text frame on the master page where you want the page number to appear, and then choose Type > Insert Special Character > Auto Page Number. Be sure to put an auto page number character on the opposite master page, as well. The keyboard shortcut is Command-Option-Shift-N (Mac OS) or Ctrl-Alt-Shift-N (Windows).

## Numbering Options

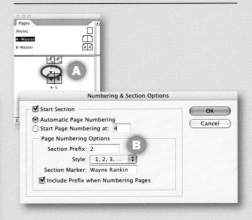

Often, the introduction to a book is numbered using Roman numerals, and the main body of the book uses Arabic numerals. In fact, the numbering typically starts over for the body of the book. To set the page-numbering style for a section of your document, double-click the triangle **A** over the page icon for the first page in the section in the Pages palette. Then, in the Numbering & Sections dialog box **B**, choose a numbering style and specify which number to start with. (If Auto Page Numbering is selected, InDesign continues numbering from the previous section.)

## Creating New Sections

## Assigning a Section Prefix and Section Marker

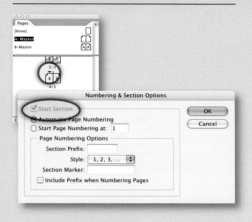

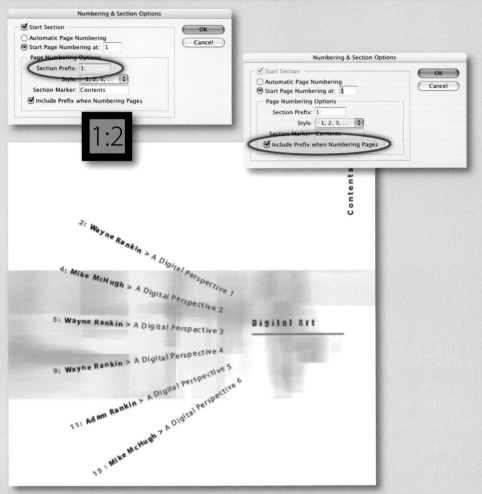

It's easier to lay out chapters of a book if you've created sections in your document. By default, each document has one section. To divide it into additional sections, select the page icon in the Pages palette for the first page in the section you want to create. Then choose Numbering and Sections from the Pages palette menu. In the New Section dialog box select Start Section. It's really that simple. Now a little triangle will appear over the first page of the section in the Pages palette.

One of the benefits of using sections in InDesign is that you can customize the headers and footers in your document more easily. For example, you can add a section prefix to the page number (such as Appendix A), or add a section marker at the top of the page (such as Chapter 2 or Wayne Rankin). To specify a section prefix and marker, double-click the triangle for the section, and then enter a prefix

and marker in the Numbering & Section Options dialog box. To apply a prefix, select "Include Prefix when Numbering Pages." To apply a section marker, create a text frame where you want it to appear, click an insertion point, and then choose Type > Insert Special Character > Section Marker. The text you specified will automatically appear there on the page. ▥

# 4

# TABLES

*Sorting Out Difficult
and Sometimes Boring
Information and
Making It Look Great*

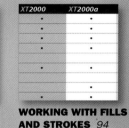

**P**SST . . . WAKE UP. Don't nod off just yet. We know that tables are usually a great way to beat insomnia, better than counting sheep. But the tables in this chapter are like counting tap-dancing sheep that are colored hot pink, wear roller skates, sing, and have laser beams attached to their heads, Doctor Evil style.

That's right, folks. Within the next few pages, we have sexed up tables. Many people said it could not be done, but with the aid of the great table features in InDesign and creative use of images and colors, we take some simple information and convert it into a visual table spectacular.

### Data, Data Everywhere

Before we get too excited, we first have to get the table information into the document. Zzzz . . . We hear you, but really, it's not that bad. You may have slabs of information supplied as tabbed

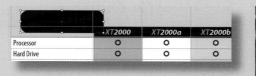

text, a Microsoft Excel table, or, worse still, tables inside a Microsoft Word document. There's no need to fear. We show you how to place that information into InDesign and start massaging it into a tasteful treat of a table.

InDesign gives you flexibility, too, whether you're starting with tabbed text, creating a table from scratch, or importing something that's already been partially formatted. We'll help you get your data in smoothly, in the most efficient way possible.

### Design Feats

If you have ever had to use tabs to set up any sort of table, in a financial report or a comparison chart or anything else, we know your pain. Studying the simple

tips we provide and understanding how to use the table features themselves not only can save you many hours in time—it may actually preserve your sanity.

With the skills you'll learn here, you can stop worrying about tabs and start creating innovative, interesting tables. That's the whole reason you're creating tables in InDesign, right? After all, if we left the design work to a word processor, it would likely fall to some sort of wizard. And as a general rule, anything with the word *wizard* in its name isn't worth using.

We know that good designers don't like to be restricted by the limitations of software. Therefore, we tackle some of the demands that designers place on InDesign and its tables. We highlight some extra tricks you can do with tables that you may not have realized were possible—things like rounded corners and images cropped within cells. Don't be a slave to the software. Bend it to suit your needs and don't compromise. Our hope is that a few of the tips in this chapter can give you the confidence and freedom you need to jump at the chance to design a table, instead of running in the other direction.

# Creating Tables in InDesign

Tables in InDesign CS2 are not the dreary things you may have experienced in other applications. The table feature draws tidy, flexible cell-based tables that make importing the data easy and customizing it fun. Just remember that tables always go in text frames, and you use the Type tool to edit them.

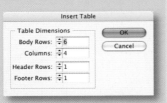

## Inserting a New Table

You can create a new table anywhere you want it in an InDesign document. Just draw a text frame, click the Type tool in it, and choose Table > Insert Table. Then specify how many rows, columns, header rows, and footer rows your table should have, and click OK. InDesign creates a table grid with independent cells. Type your data in each cell, and then tab to the next.

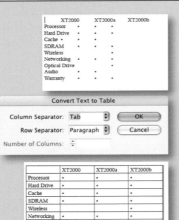

## Creating a Table from Existing Text

Sometimes you already have the table data in your document, formatted with tabs or commas. (This is sometimes called *tab-delimited* or *comma-delimited* text.) If someone's provided the data this way, you're halfway there. Just select the text and choose Table > Convert Text to Table. In the Convert Text to Table dialog box, choose either the tab character, the comma, or, in rare cases, the paragraph return as the cell separator. Usually, you'll also want to specify that a paragraph return indicates a new row. When you click OK, InDesign converts your text into a tidy new table, ready for formatting.

> **T I P**
>
> **Show Hidden Characters.** If you're not certain whether your text is tab-delimited, choose Type > Show Hidden Characters. InDesign displays all the tabs, spaces, paragraph returns, and other hidden characters in your text. Each tab appears as two small greater-than signs (>>).

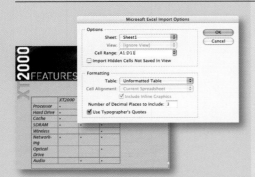

## Importing an Excel File for a Table

It's easy to pull an Excel file into an InDesign table—and you don't have to know anything about Excel! Create a text frame for the table, and click an insertion point with the Type tool. Next, choose File > Place, select the Excel file, select Show Import Options, and then click Open. Then, in the Microsoft Excel Import Options dialog box, choose the cell range (with A1 being the top-left cell) that you want to import. Choose whether you want to keep the table's formatting, or even to import it as tabbed text. If you import it as a formatted or unformatted table, InDesign immediately places it into a table grid.

# Customizing a Table

*Once you've created your table, there are many ways that you can customize it to fit the design of your document. In this section, we'll focus on perfecting the basic size of the table's cells, and on formatting the text.*

### 1. Move the Cell Borders.

When you first create your table, the cell borders may not be quite where you want them for the design of your page. To move the borders, drag them with the Type tool. If you first create guides where you want the borders to be, InDesign will snap the borders to the guides as you drag the borders near them.

## 2. Delete Extra Rows or Columns.

In most cases, empty rows or columns clutter the look of a table. If you overestimated the number of rows or columns you'd need or you imported an Excel file that included empty rows or columns, delete them. First select the row or column. To select a row, move the pointer to the far left edge of the row until it turns into an arrow pointing to the right, and then click **A**. To select a column, move the pointer to the top edge of the column until it becomes an arrow pointing down, and then click **B**. Once the row or column is selected, press Command-Delete (Mac OS) or Ctrl-Backspace (Windows) to delete it.

---

**T I P**

**Drag to Select.** If you don't want to edit an entire row or column, click in the first cell you want to edit and drag across to include all the cells you want to select.

## 3. Format All the Text in a Row or Column.

The text in your table is editable, so you could select each character and apply formatting to it. However, you can also select the entire cell, row, column, or table, and apply text formatting to all of it at once. In this case, we'll apply paragraph styles to different rows in the table. Select the Type tool, and then select the first row and apply a paragraph style. Do the same for each row in the table. We've applied the Product Names style to the first row, and Feature Names to the other rows.

### 4. Format Individual Paragraphs in a Cell.

It's quick to apply formatting to several cells at once, but sometimes you want to treat portions of a cell differently. To apply paragraph styles or other formatting to individual paragraphs, words, or characters in a cell, select the text, and then either apply a paragraph or character style or manually format the text.

### 5. Apply Color to Text in Cells.

You can create stronger distinctions between sections of your table, or simply make a fashion statement, by coloring the text. Coloring the text in a table is just like coloring the text in any other text frame: Select the cell or cells whose contents you want to color, click the Text icon in the Color palette or the Toolbox, and then select a color from the Swatches palette. InDesign applies the color to the selected text.

### 6. Align Text.

You can apply other text-formatting attributes, such as alignment. For example, if you want to center bullets in a table, select their cells, and then click the center alignment option in the Control palette.

# Working with Fills and Strokes

Let's face it: Black-and-white tables are boring. Unless you're creating a modernistic masterpiece, you'll want to add color to your tables. You can use color to help readers identify different columns or sections of the table—or just to keep them interested while they pore over a set of statistics.

## Reversing Text

Reversed text looks sharp, particularly in a table heading. First, color your text white. Now, obviously, if you've got white text on a light-colored background, it won't show up. If your borders are black, though, it's easy to create a black background for your text. Just select the cells, and then flip the Fill and Stroke values in the Toolbox.

> **T I P**
>
> **Quick Flip.** To switch the Fill and Stroke values quickly, press Shift-X.

## Selecting Vertical and Horizontal Lines

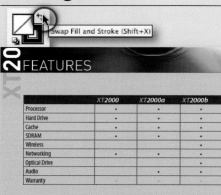

When you select multiple cells in a table, InDesign adds a table proxy to the right side of the Control palette. The proxy represents the grid lines in your table. To select a line in your table, select the entire table, and then select the line in the proxy and deselect the ones you don't want to affect. By default, all the lines in the proxy are selected.

> **T I P**
>
> **Seeing Grid Lines.** If you've snapped the cell borders to guides, those same guides may be blocking your view of the lines. To see the lines, switch to Preview mode, or choose View > Grids & Guides > Hide Guides.

## Changing the Color and Weight of a Stroke

Once you've selected the vertical or horizontal lines in the proxy, you can edit or even remove them. Choose a weight and pattern for the stroke from the menu next to the grid. If you don't want a line to appear at all, choose 0 for the stroke width, or click the Stroke icon

in the Toolbox and then click the Apply None icon. To add a color to a line, select it in the proxy and then click a swatch in the Swatches palette.

**T I P**

**Start Over.** To deselect all the lines in the proxy and begin fresh, just triple-click the proxy.

## Changing Fill Colors Manually

You can change the fill, or background, color in table cells. First, select the cells you want to change. Then click the Fill icon in the Toolbox to make it active, and select a color in the Swatches palette. You can apply any color in the Swatches palette, and you can create tints, as well. ▥

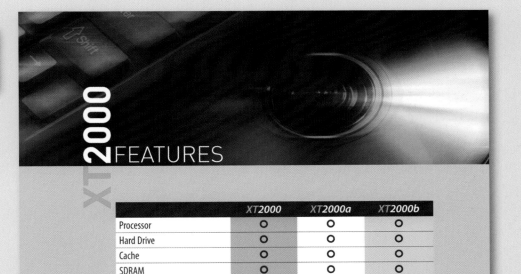

| | XT2000 | XT2000a | XT2000b |
|---|---|---|---|
| Processor | ○ | ○ | ○ |
| Hard Drive | ○ | ○ | ○ |
| Cache | ○ | ○ | ○ |
| SDRAM | ○ | ○ | ○ |
| Wireless | | | ○ |
| Networking | ○ | ○ | ○ |
| Optical Drive | | | ○ |
| Audio | | ○ | ○ |
| Warranty | ○ | ○ | • |

# Using Images in Tables

**Tables don't have to be filled with boring text. Sometimes images can make a table more interesting or make a concept clearer. Use images you've created in other applications, or copy and paste a graphic you've drawn in InDesign.**

**1. Set Cell Options.**

Before adding images, it's best to set up your cell parameters so that they behave as you expect. First, select the cells into which you want to paste a graphic. Then choose Table > Cell Options and choose the Text tab. Because you want to fill the cell, set the inset values to 0 **A**. To ensure that it lands where you expect, change the First Baseline Offset to Fixed **B** with an appropriate minimum value. We've used 10 mm in our example. Finally, because you don't want the image spilling over into other cells, select Clip Contents to Cell **C**.

## 2. Paste the Image into the Cell.

What could be easier than copying and pasting? Copy or cut the image you want to paste into the first cell and then click in that cell with the Type tool and paste the image. We owe our wonderful sample photographs to Adam Rankin, Wayne's son.

## 3. Crop the Image Frame.

The image is automatically cropped to fit into the cell when you paste it, but its frame isn't. First, we need to pull the image down into its cell, and then, to keep things tidy, we recommend that you crop the image frame. Use the Selection tool to drag the image into position and then to crop the frame to the edge of the cell.

## 4. Position the Image.

You can fuss with the image even after it's in the cell. To position it precisely within its frame, drag it with the Direct Selection tool.

# Creating a Rounded-Corner Effect

Here's a more advanced trick for you to help your table stand out from the crowd. We'll add a rounded edge to the upper-left corner of a table.

**1. Remove Formatting from the Cell.**
We'll eventually be pasting a rectangle with rounded corners into the first cell of this table **A**. To keep from compli-cating things, let's start by removing the existing formatting from that cell. The only formatting in this cell in our sample table is a black fill. We'll just select the cell with the Type tool, click the Fill icon in the Toolbox, and then click Apply None to empty the cell **B**.

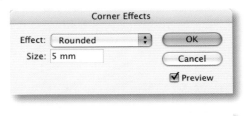

## 2. Set Cell Options.

We'll be pasting a rectangle into this cell, so we want to make sure the cell is set up properly. With the cell selected, choose Table > Cell Options and click the Text tab. By default, an inset is applied. To make the rectangle go to the edge of the cell, we'll change the inset values to 0. Additionally, select Clip Contents to Cell so that the rectangle won't overlap into other cells. And, finally, choose where the first baseline will start; in this case, we'll set the baseline offset at Fixed and type *5 mm* for the minimum, so that we'll be able to click and drag the rounded rectangle in that cell.

## 3. Draw a Rectangle with Rounded Corners.

With the Rectangle tool, draw a rectangle approximately the size of the cell it will go in. (You can resize it later.) For this example, we'll add a black fill to match the rest of the heading row. Now, to round the corners, choose Object > Corner Effects. Choose Rounded in the Corner Effects dialog box. You can select Preview to see what the result will be. We'll set it at 5 mm, because that looks right for this table, and then click OK.

## 4. Paste the Rectangle into the Cell.

Now to get that rectangle into the cell: Cut or copy it to the clipboard. Then select the Type tool, click in the first cell, and paste in the rectangle.

## 5. Position the Rectangle.

We only want the upper-left corner of the rectangle to show, so that it rounds out the corner of our entire table. Therefore, we need to position it carefully. Drag it out so that the only visible corner is the upper-left corner, and the others are all clipped by the edges of the cell. We'll also shorten the top row to get a sleeker look. ▥

# 5

# USING COLOR IN INDESIGN DOCUMENTS

*Adding Pizzazz to Any Design and Getting the Results You Want*

**D**ESIGNERS USE COLORS the way musicians use instruments, to create a mood and set the tone for a document. But deciding which colors to use is only the first step. Once you've chosen the colors, things can get a little trickier. We've pulled together tips and techniques that should keep you in a good mood, whether you're setting a jovial tone with bright primary colors, a casual style with earthy browns, ochres, and greens, or something completely different.

### Take Your Pick of Methods

There are as many approaches to working with InDesign as there are designers. To help you find your own favorite path, we introduce you to several ways to apply color to objects and text, working with the Swatches palette, Color palette, and Toolbox. You can drag and drop a color, use the Eyedropper, or select swatches in palettes. Mix the colors up a bit by using gradients or by combining inks.

It's important that color falls where you want it to, so we show you how to apply color to fills and strokes separately—even when coloring text. And we help you get the job done more efficiently with shortcuts and tips.

### Getting Results

Many folks enjoy applying color to documents but dread sending their files to print, afraid that objects will print on the wrong plate or the color won't print as expected. We recognize those jitters. The good news is that you needn't dread print time if you plan for it as you go.

If you're designing a job that will be printed commercially, communicate with the printer and your client ahead of time. Determine whether you'll be using spot or process colors, whether you should use specific Pantone colors, and how you'll handle varnishes and other special effects.

Once you've answered the basic questions, follow our guidelines to set up Pantone swatches and to create spot colors for special printing needs, such as varnishes and die lines. For tight printing budgets, we show you how to be thrifty and get the most out of a two-color job.

Before you print, use the Separations Preview palette in InDesign to see exactly how your plates will print. This fabulous palette saves you frustration and money. And because it removes the need to run test separations for even the trickiest print jobs, it also helps you save some trees. Not bad for one little palette, eh?

### Step Out of the Pack

After a while, CMYK four-color process jobs all start to look alike. If you want your design to stand out, take advantage of InDesign features to add spot colors, varnishes, and special inks—and to use overprinting to good effect. We work on a custom wine bottle label in this chapter that shows how these touches can make all the difference.

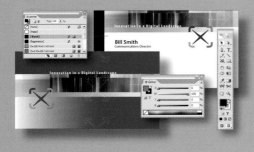

# About Color and Swatches

There are several ways to accomplish almost any task in InDesign, and working with color is no exception. You can apply color to objects in your document using the Toolbox, Swatches palette, or Color palette, depending on your preference. Regardless of your workflow, to use color effectively, you also need to choose the appropriate color mode and know how to set defaults.

## Color Modes

Which color mode you use depends on your output goals. For high-end printing, you'll typically use CMYK. However, if you're creating PDF files to be distributed online or on a CD, RGB may be more appropriate. Just as in Adobe Photoshop and Illustrator, you need to choose a color mode in InDesign, especially if you're using transparency. To specify a color mode for transparency, choose Edit > Transparency Blend Space, and then choose Document RGB or Document CMYK.

## Toolbox

The bottom section of the Toolbox contains several options related to color. The solid square and outlined square represent the fill **A** and stroke **B**, respectively, of the selected object; if no object is selected, they display the defaults. Other icons let you apply color to the text frame **C** or the text it contains **D**, apply a gradient **E**, or remove a fill or stroke (apply none) **F**.

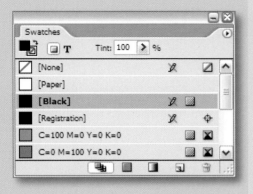

## Swatches Palette

The Swatches palette gives you complete control over all the colors, tints, and gradients in your document. You can add swatches to increase your color options in InDesign. Additionally, you can use the Fill and Stroke icons to apply color to objects, or apply color to text or its container.

**T I P**

**Default Swatches.** To change the swatches that appear by default in new documents, edit the Swatches palette when no documents are open.

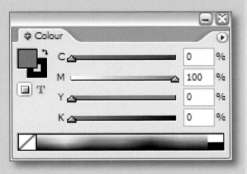

## Color Palette

The Color palette doesn't list the available colors; instead, it provides a mixing board for you to create your own new swatches. It contains many of the icons for applying color that appear in the Toolbox and the Swatches palette.

**I N S I G H T**

**Connected Tools.** The same icons for fill, stroke, text, and object appear in the Toolbox, Swatches palette, and Color palette. When you select one of these icons in any one of these places, it is instantly selected in the others; they mirror each other. For example, if you select the stroke in the Swatches palette, it's automatically selected in the Color palette and the Toolbox. As you'll have the same result no matter which you choose, use the one that feels most natural to you.

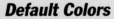

## Default Colors

When you type or draw a shape in an InDesign document, InDesign automatically applies the default color for fill, stroke, text, and container. To change the default for a document, make sure you have nothing selected on the page, and then select a fill, stroke, text, or container color or setting. To change the default for all new documents you create in InDesign, close all documents and then select a setting. ▦

# Adding Swatches

**Create your own CMYK, RGB, spot, or process color swatches in InDesign, or use colors from a professional color library, such as the Pantone libraries.**

## 1. Choose New Color Swatch.

To add a color swatch to your swatches palette, first choose New Color Swatch from the Swatches palette menu **A**. Alternatively, you can press Option (Mac OS) or Alt (Windows) and click the New Color Swatch icon **B** at the bottom of the palette. InDesign opens the New Color Swatch dialog box.

## 2. Choose a Color Type.

Process colors are created on the press by combining the cyan, magenta, yellow, and black plates. If you're working on a full-color job with photographs or other subtle color variations, you may want to use process colors. However, if you want to ensure that a color is exactly what you expect, use a spot color, which will be applied on its own plate. Choose Process or Spot from the Color Type menu. In our example, we're creating a Pantone color that we want to print on its own plate, so we'll choose Spot.

### 3. Choose a Color Mode or Color Library.

If you're creating your own color, specify whether it's RGB or CMYK, and then move the sliders to create the color you want to use. If you want to use a color from a Pantone library or another color library, choose the library from the Color Mode menu. Here, we'll choose the "Pantone solid coated" library.

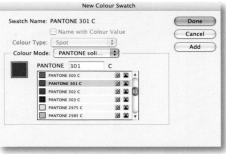

### 4. If You're Using a Library, Select the Color.

You can type in the color number you want to use, if you know it, or scroll through the library and select the color you want to use. We'll select Pantone 301, a nice blue color.

### 5. Add the Swatch.

Once you've selected the color from the color library or defined and named a color of your own, click Add. InDesign adds the swatch to the Swatches palette. You can then apply the color to any objects on the page, and it will be included in any list of swatches, such as the gap color in the Strokes palette.

### 6. Add More Swatches.

If you're using a library, you can continue to select additional colors, and then click Add to add each one to your Swatches palette. If you're defining your own colors, you can define additional colors, as long as you name them differently, and add them to the Swatches palette, as well. Let's add 157, 165, and 354 to our Swatches palette.

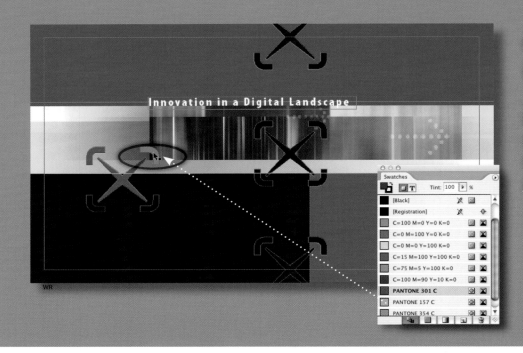

# Applying Color to Objects and Text

*Easily apply color to the stroke or fill of objects or text, using whichever method you prefer.*

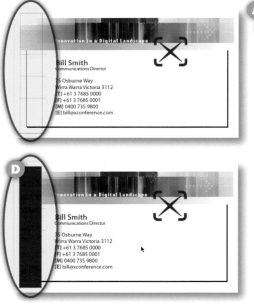

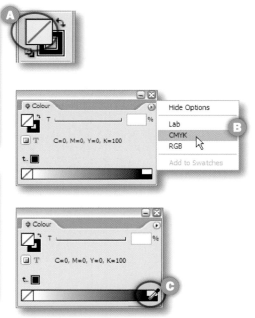

**1. Change the Fill Color for an Object.**
We're creating a business card that already contains several objects, but we need to add a rectangle. Using the Rectangle tool, draw a rectangle out to the red bleed line outside the page and to the guide we've already created. By default, our stroke is black and there is no fill. Let's change the fill to black. Select the rectangle with the Selection tool. Click the Fill icon in the Toolbox **A** to make it active. Then choose CMYK from the Color palette menu **B**. Finally, click the black rectangle at the far-right end of the color bar in the Color palette **C**. Now we've got a rectangle with a black fill and a black stroke **D**.

## 2. Remove the Stroke Color.

We want this rectangle to have a black fill and no stroke, so we need to remove the stroke. Select the object with the Selection tool. Click the Stroke icon to make it active **A**. Then click the Apply None icon in the Toolbox **B**, or select None in the Swatches palette. InDesign removes the stroke.

## 3. Apply Color to Text.

At the top of the business card, there's a strip of text that appears white. When we select the text frame with the Selection tool, the icons in the Toolbox, Swatches palette, and Color palette indicate that it has no fill and no stroke. That's because the text *frame* has no fill or stroke applied; the text itself, however, clearly has Paper color applied. You might think we'd have to select the text with the Type tool to color it, but in InDesign CS2, we can just click the T icon in the Toolbox, Swatches palette, or Color palette to apply color to text. When we click that icon, we see a Paper color fill and no stroke. If we were to click Black in the Swatches palette, the text would become black.

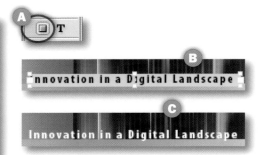

### 4. Apply Color to the Text Frame.

We can apply color to the text frame separately from the text. Click the Formatting Affects Container icon **A** in the Toolbox, Swatches palette, or Color palette. Now we'll affect the fill and stroke of the frame itself. Click the yellow color in the Swatches palette to fill the frame **B**. If we decide that yellow is a little too bright, we can easily click None in the Swatches palette to remove the fill from the frame. And because the black text doesn't show up all that well, let's select the T icon again, and then select Paper in the Swatches palette to make our text white again **C**.

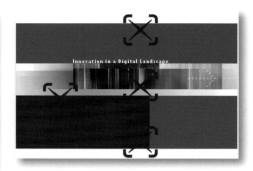

### 5. Drag and Drop Swatches.

Now we'll add color to the logo on this business card. We'll use one of the Pantone colors we added to the Swatches palette, PANTONE 301. We could select the logo and then select the swatch, but instead we'll drag and drop. Just drag the PANTONE 301 swatch onto the middle of the X. The cursor has a little plus sign on it. Release the mouse button and the X is blue. We can drag and drop color onto the four corners of our logo, as well. Let's drop 301 onto the top-left corner, 165 onto the top-right corner, 157 onto the bottom-left corner, and 354 onto the bottom-right corner.

We've got plenty of work to do on the back of the business card. Click the Go to Last Page button at the bottom of the document to switch to the back of the card. Then we'll color in the background by dragging and dropping the PANTONE 301 swatch for a lovely blue color.

## 6. Use the Direct Selection Tool.

There are several copies of the logo on the back of the card, and each of them is grouped. We'll apply the same colors we used on the front of the card to the logo on the far left. But this time, let's use the Direct Selection tool to assign a color to each section of the logo. First, select the Direct Selection tool **A**. Then select the middle X **B**, and select PANTONE 301 in the Swatches palette **C**. We'll use the Direct Selection tool to apply 301 to the top-left corner as well, and then to apply 165 to the top-right corner, 157 to the bottom-left corner, and 354 to the bottom-right corner.

## 7. Use the Eyedropper Tool.

You've already learned several ways to apply color in InDesign, but there's yet another method! You can use the Eyedropper tool to sample colors and apply them elsewhere. First, we'll drag the Paper color onto the X in the middle logo. That's the color we want to apply to all three of these logos. Now, select the Eyedropper tool, which we think looks quite a bit like a turkey baster. Then, click the paper-colored X to fill the Eyedropper. It flips over to indicate that it's full. Finally, click in each shape we want to apply the color to. In this case, we'll click in each of the four corners of this middle logo, and then in each of the five shapes in the top and bottom logos. The Eyedropper tool is a great tool to use if you want to apply the same color to several different objects quickly.

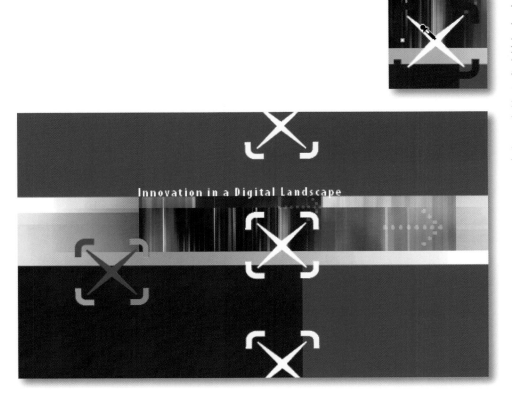

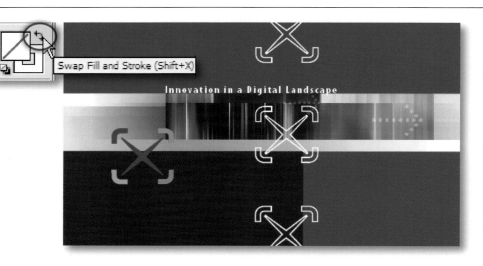

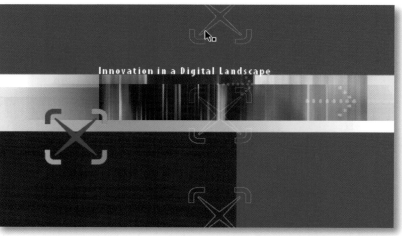

### 8. Switch Stroke and Fill.

The logo shapes each have a fill of Paper and a stroke of none. We'd like to change that so that each has only a paper-colored keyline. Select all three logos. To switch the fill and stroke colors, click the Swap Fill and Stroke icon (a curved double arrow) in the Toolbox, or press Shift-X. Now we have three logos with paper-colored strokes and no fills. Now that we have our keylines in place, we'll decrease the stroke weight a little bit: In the Strokes palette, change the weight to .25 and press Enter. ▥

**Question Mark.** The Stroke and Fill icons in the Toolbox, Color palette, and Swatches palette change to represent the color actually applied to the stroke and fill in the selected object. Therefore, if you select multiple objects that have different colors applied, those Stroke and Fill icons contain question marks. If you apply a color to all the selected objects, the question marks are replaced with that color.

**Fill to Stroke, Stroke to Fill.** To make the Fill icon active, you can select it, of course, or you can simply press the X key. When it's active, press the X key again to switch to the Stroke icon. To switch the values of the fill and stroke, press Shift-X. These shortcuts work no matter what tool you have selected, or what you're doing in the application.

# Working with Tints

Use tints to add depth and interest to a one-color or two-color document, or simply to get just the mood you want.

## Creating a Tint Swatch

When you select a swatch in the Swatches palette, the Color palette slider displays a gradient from white to the full swatch color. To specify a tint of 50%, type *50* in the percentage field. Then click the tinted icon in the Color palette and drag it to the Swatches palette. Now you can apply the tint swatch as you would any other swatch.

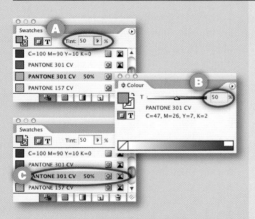

## Applying a Tint to an Object

There are several ways to apply a tint to an object. First, select the object you want to tint, and apply the full color swatch to it. Then, type a percentage value in the Tint field in the Swatches palette A or next to the slider in the Color palette B. Or, if you've already created a tint swatch, just click the swatch in the Swatches palette C.

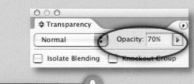

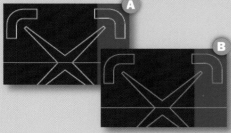

## Applying Transparency

You can also achieve a tint effect by blending an object with its background. Select the object, apply the full-color swatch, and then change the Opacity value in the Transparency palette. In this example, the first logo is at 100% opacity A, and the second logo is at 70% opacity B. As always, the effect you achieve using the Transparency palette depends on the blending mode you use. Here, we've used Normal mode. ▥

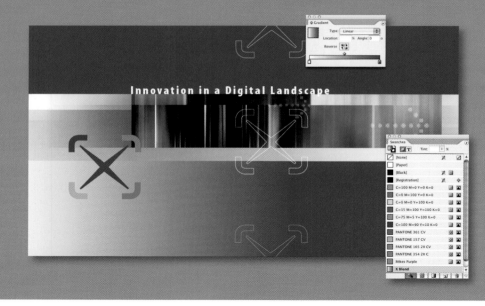

# Working with Gradients

*Apply gradients to objects in your page directly in InDesign, without having to use Adobe Illustrator or any other application.*

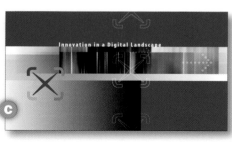
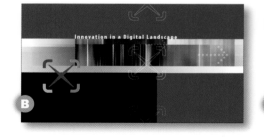

### 1. Apply a Gradient.

It's simple to apply a gradient to an object in InDesign CS2. First select the object you want to apply a gradient to, and then click the Apply Gradient icon in the Toolbox **A**. Here, we'll apply a gradient to the rectangle in the lower-left corner of the back of the business card. What was a black rectangle **B** now begins white and gradually becomes darker until it's full black on the right side **C**.

### 2. Adjust the Gradient.

When you first apply the gradient, InDesign applies it evenly from left to right, moving horizontally across the object. You can modify that gradient, though, to move from right to left, top to bottom, or bottom to top. You can even change the gradient distance. To adjust the gradient, click the Gradient tool where you want the gradient to begin, and then drag it across the object to where you want it to end.

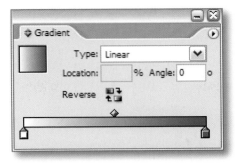

### CAUTION

**Gradient vs. Solid Color.** Make sure you press the Option (Mac OS) or Alt (Windows) key while you click the swatch you want to assign. If you click the color stop in the Gradient palette and then simply click a swatch in the Swatches palette, InDesign will apply solid color to the object.

### TIP

**Gradient of Many Colors.** A gradient doesn't have to be composed of two colors. You can create additional color stops; just click beneath the Gradient bar to create them. Then assign any swatch to each color stop, and move the color stop along the Gradient bar to change the effect.

### TIP

**Uniform Gradient.** Does your gradient sag a bit? If you want it to be perfectly horizontal, vertical, or at a 45-degree angle, press the Shift key while you drag the Gradient tool across the object.

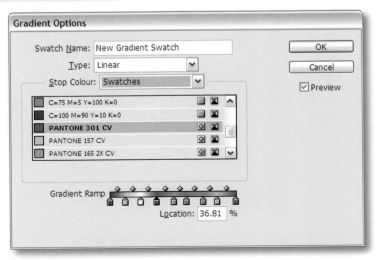

## 3. Change the Colors in the Gradient.

Gradients don't have to be black and white; you can use any colors you want. To assign a color, open the Gradient palette, click the first or last color stop in the Gradient bar, and then press the Option or Alt key while you click a swatch in the Swatches palette. Or just drag a color swatch onto the color stop. You can assign colors to both color stops, so you could have a gradient from magenta to blue, or green to red, or any combination of colors. To change the center point of the gradient, move the bar in the Gradient palette.

## 4. Save the Gradient as a Swatch.

When you create a gradient you like, save it as a swatch to use on other objects later. To save the swatch, click the gradient icon in the Gradient palette, and then drag it onto the Swatches palette and drop it. If you know exactly how you want your gradient to look, you can also create the swatch first and then apply it to objects as you would any other swatch. Just choose New Gradient Swatch from the Swatches palette menu, and then specify the name, type, and color stops for the gradient swatch. ▥

# Using Special Colors

You can create swatches that go beyond the traditional CMYK or RGB models. For example, you can create a metallic color or a varnish swatch. In our artwork, Wayne used a metallic color, PANTONE 8281, across the top of this wine bottle label, and he used a gloss varnish for the logo and a few other elements. Essentially, you can use a spot color swatch to define any process that you want to mark on a separate plate.

## *Die Line*

When you're working with a document that has an unusual shape, it's essential that the printer can find the die line easily, for the die cut. Create a swatch in a color that stands out from the rest of your document. In this case, we're using magenta. Then make sure it's a spot color, so that it will appear on its own plate. Be sure to name it Die Line so that you'll remember what it is when you're working with swatches.

## *Varnish*

A varnish swatch isn't quite like most other swatches, because a varnish isn't a color—it's a treatment. However, you create a varnish swatch just as you create color swatches. Click the New Swatch icon in the Swatches palette. Choose Spot from the Color Type menu because the varnish needs to have its own separation. You can choose any color you want for the swatch because it's just a screen representation. However, to keep it a little more lifelike, we usually use 10% yellow. Be sure to name it Varnish and to set it to overprint.

## Overprinting

When you're creating special die line or varnish swatches, you don't want them to knock out the objects beneath them. To ensure that they print as expected, set the die line and varnish areas to overprint. Choose Window > Attributes to open the Attributes palette. Then select the object you want to overprint, and select Overprint Fill and Overprint Stroke, as appropriate.

## Separations Preview

Before committing your document to film, it's a good idea to make sure everything's going to come out on the right plate. Use the Separations Preview palette in InDesign CS2 to see your separations onscreen, so that you can make any necessary adjustments. Choose Window > Output  Separations Preview to open the palette. Choose Separations from the View menu, and then select the plate you want to preview. ▥

# Mixing Inks

*Create mixed ink swatches to increase the number of colors in your document without increasing the number of separations. You can create a swatch that is a mixture of two or more spot inks, or a spot ink and one or more process inks.*

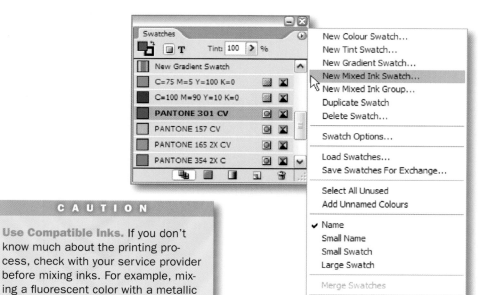

**1. Choose New Mixed Ink Swatch.**
To create a mixed ink swatch, choose New Mixed Ink Swatch from the Swatches palette menu. This option is available only if you have at least one spot color in your Swatches palette.

## New Mixed Ink Swatch

**Name:** Pantone 174 with gloss

Inks

| | Process Cyan | | % |
| | Process Magenta | | % |
| | Process Yellow | | % |
| | Process Black | | % |
| | PANTONE 8281 C | | % |
| | PANTONE 174 C | 100 % |
| | gloss Varnish | 100 % |

[OK] [Cancel] [Add]

## 2. Select the Colors to Mix.

The New Mixed Ink Swatch dialog box lists all the colors available for mixing from your Swatches palette. Select the colors you want to mix, and then specify a percentage for each of the colors. The dialog box displays a preview of the mixed ink swatch so that you can see how it changes as you increase or decrease the percentages. Remember, though, that a screen representation of a color may not show you how the color will actually print.

Name the swatch so that you'll remember when you intended to use it. Then click Add if you want to create more mixed swatches, or click OK to add just this one to the Swatches palette.

### INSIGHT

**Automatic Varnish.** If you know you'll always want to apply varnish over a specific color in your document, create a mixed ink swatch with those two swatches. Then you can save yourself some steps as you apply them at once—and you won't have to worry that you've forgotten to varnish an object.

## Swatches

Tint: 100 %

| PANTONE 8281 C | |
| PANTONE 174 C | |
| gloss Varnish | |
| Die Line | |
| Pantone 174 with varnish | |

## 3. Apply the Swatch.

InDesign treats mixed ink swatches like any other swatches in your palette. To apply the swatch, you can drag and drop it onto an object, or select an object and then select the swatch. When you apply it, InDesign automatically applies all of the selected inks at the percentages you specified. If you want to verify how the inks are getting separated, use the Separations Preview palette to see each plate.

### INSIGHT

**Mixed Ink Group.** In addition to a mixed ink swatch, you can create a mixed ink group, which is a series of colors that combine the inks you selected in different percentages, at the increment you specify. For example, you could mix different tints of cyan with various tints of a spot color for a whole range of swatches, all in one mixed ink group. To create a mixed ink group, choose New Mixed Ink Group from the Swatches palette.

### New Mixed Ink Group

**Name:** Group 1

Inks

| | | Initial | Repeat | Increment |
| | Process Black | | | |
| | PANTONE 8281 C | 5% | 5 | 10% |
| | PANTONE 174 C | 5% | 5 | 20% |
| | gloss Varnish | | | |
| | Die Line | | | |

Included Inks: PANTONE 8281 C, PANTONE 174 C

Swatches to be Generated: 36   [Preview Swatches]

Swatch Preview

| Group 1 Swatch 1 |
| Group 1 Swatch 2 |
| Group 1 Swatch 3 |
| Group 1 Swatch 4 |
| Group 1 Swatch 5 |

[OK] [Cancel]

# 6

# IMPORTING GRAPHICS

*Placing, Manipulating—
Even Modifying—Artwork
from Other Applications*

**I**MAGINE THE CONVERSATION that the Adobe InDesign developers had when it came time to choose the default keyboard shortcut for the Place command. "Well, we can't use Command-P. The dudes over in the Print office have bagged that one for the foreseeable future." "Yeah, and the Group team won't budge on Command-G. I thought that would be perfect, G as in Get!" "No, no, no! Smithy, did you have any luck with Marketing and Legal? Can we use E, like Quark does?" "Nah, they won't budge. Elliot was working on that and then he up and moved to Australia, of all places. I don't think they even have computers there yet, do they? Anyway, E is for Export." "Well, I'm tired and hungry. What's available? D? OK, that's it. Command-D it is. Let's go home."

We can't tell you why Adobe chose D as the keyboard shortcut for the Place command, but in this chapter, we help you make sense of everything else you need to know about bringing outside artwork into InDesign and working with it effectively. You don't need to draw a frame before you place an image in InDesign,

but you do need to know how to crop, scale, and reposition it once you've got it in the document.

### The Link to Power

Key to the power of placed graphics—that is, graphics you import using the Place command—are the links InDesign creates for them. Links let you store your large graphic files outside the document, keeping the file size down, while enabling you to ensure that you're using the latest version of a graphic. We'll show you how to manage those links, and we'll introduce you to some of the features in the Links palette that designers sometimes overlook.

One of the important benefits of links is that they give you the opportunity to modify objects even after you've placed them in your document. InDesign's support for a wide variety of file formats lets you make changes to original

artwork from other applications at any stage of the project, seamlessly, using the enhanced Edit Original feature.

### The InDesign Advantage

InDesign has one huge advantage over other page-layout applications: the ability to place native Adobe Photoshop and Illustrator files, as well as PDF files. This affords us much more flexibility when we construct and design our pages. We explore these options in detail and encourage you to leave behind the old workflow of flattening Photoshop files and saving them as EPS graphics to place in your layout. We also look closely at working with Illustrator, including the benefits you can gain by copying and pasting simple paths into InDesign.

We'll show you how to get the most out of all the new formats in the Adobe Creative Suite 2 applications, without ever having to resort to EPS files. For example, you can retain clipping paths and spot colors in native Photoshop files; saving the images as EPS files first would only slow you down.

Enjoy the new workflow, as you and InDesign boldly go where no page-layout application has gone before.

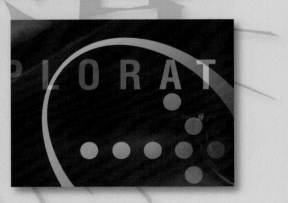

# Placing an Image

*The Place command is where the action is in InDesign. Placing a graphic into InDesign creates a link to the original file so that the graphic prints appropriately—and so that you can edit or update it.*

**1. Choose File > Place.**

Unlike QuarkXPress and some other page-layout applications, InDesign doesn't require you to create a frame on the page before you choose the Place command. Choose File > Place, or press Command-D (Mac OS) or Ctrl-D (Windows).

**2. Select the File You Want to Place.**

Select the file you want to import. InDesign can import many different graphic formats, including native Illustrator and Photoshop files. You can also place pages from Adobe PDF files as graphics. We'll place Rocks.psd, a photograph that Wayne Rankin took in Tasmania, to use as the background for our CD advertisement.

To see all the options associated with the format you're using, select Show Import Options. If you've selected an object you want to replace with the graphic, also select Replace Selected Item. And then click Open.

## 3. Select File Import Options.

The import options you see depend on the graphic format of the file you're importing. In our example, we're importing a Photoshop file, so we could include the Photoshop clipping path, if there were one in the photo. There's also a Color tab, so that we can enable color management and choose the profile and rendering intent for this file. If we were placing an Illustrator file, Adobe PDF, EPS, TIFF, or other format, we'd see different options. We'll accept the defaults and click OK.

## 4. Place the Image on the Page.

Click the loaded image cursor **A**, which looks like a paintbrush, in the upper-left corner of the page, to create a background. InDesign automatically creates a frame for the image. If, instead, you wanted to place the image inside an existing frame, you could just click inside the frame (the loaded image cursor changes when you hover inside a frame **B**).

If you select a frame before you place the object, InDesign automatically places it into the frame you selected. You won't see the loaded image cursor at all—but then, you won't need it. 🔲

# Positioning an Image

Once you've placed an image, you can move, crop, or resize it to fit precisely where you need it on the page. Use the Selection tool to manipulate the frame, the Direct Selection tool to maneuver the image, and the Fitting command to change the relationship between the two.

## Move an Image and Its Frame

Click an image with the Selection tool, and then just drag it where you want to position it on the page. As long as you click in the middle of the image, away from the handles, you'll move both the image and the frame without resizing either.

## Crop an Image

To make the frame smaller, thereby cropping the image it contains, click and drag a corner or side handle with the Selection tool. The entire image remains in InDesign, but the only area that previews onscreen or prints when you output the document is the portion within the frame.

### INSIGHT

**Patient User Mode.** Sometimes when you click and drag an object, you see only a sketchy outline, but other times you see a faint version of the entire object. What makes the difference? How InDesign displays the object you're moving depends on how long you keep the mouse button still before you move it. Click and hold for half a second or more before dragging if you want to see the full object. Now you know why it's called "patient user mode"!

## Reposition an Image Within Its Frame

To move the image within the frame, use the Direct Selection tool. The cursor turns into a hand. When you click the image, InDesign displays the edges of the full image, so you know how much wiggle room you have.

## Resize an Image Without Resizing Its Frame

To resize the image itself without affecting the frame, use the Direct Selection tool. Click the image, and then drag the image handle. Hold down the Shift key to resize the image proportionally. If you're resizing a raster image, such as a photograph, remember to consider the resolution of the image as you resize it. When you make an image larger, you reduce the number of pixels per inch, which reduces the image quality to most output devices.

## Fitting the Image to the Frame

| Object | |
|---|---|
| Transform | ▶ |
| Transform Again | ▶ |
| Arrange | ▶ |
| Select | ▶ |
| Group | Ctrl+G |
| Ungroup | Shift+Ctrl+G |
| Lock Position | Ctrl+L |
| Unlock Position | Alt+Ctrl+L |
| Text Frame Options... | Ctrl+B |
| Anchored Object | ▶ |
| Fitting | ▶ |
| Content | ▶ |
| Drop Shadow... | Alt+Ctrl+M |
| Feather... | |
| Corner Effects... | |
| Object Layer Options... | |
| Clipping Path... | Alt+Shift+Ctrl+K |
| Image Colour Settings... | |
| Interactive | ▶ |
| Compound Paths | ▶ |
| Paths | ▶ |
| Pathfinder | ▶ |
| Convert Shape | ▶ |
| Display Performance | ▶ |

Fitting submenu:
| | |
|---|---|
| Fit Content to Frame | Alt+Ctrl+E |
| Fit Frame to Content | Alt+Ctrl+C |
| Centre Content | Shift+Ctrl+E |
| Fit Content Proportionally | Alt+Shift+Ctrl+E |
| Fill Frame Proportionally | Alt+Shift+Ctrl+C |

You can resize an image to match a frame, create a frame the size of the full image, or center the content in the frame. Once the image is in the frame, select it with the Selection tool, and then choose Object > Fitting, and choose the command you want. ▥

---

**T I P**

**Scale Changes.** To see how much you've scaled an image when you resize it, look at the percentages in the Control palette. To see how you've affected the resolution of the image, select it and open the Info palette. There, you can see how many pixels per inch are present.

56.08%
56.08%

Info
X: -158.5 mm    W: 38.696 mm
Y: -152.5 mm    H: 41.5 mm
D:

Type: Photoshop
Actual ppi: 225x225
Effective ppi: 401x401
Colour Space: RGB
ICC Profile: Adobe RGB (1998)

# The Links Palette

The Links palette gives you one-stop shopping when you want to relink, update, edit, or simply check on the graphics you've imported.

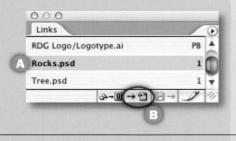

## Finding Graphics in a Document

In a lengthy document, you may not even know where a specific graphic was placed. To locate a placed object, select it in the Links palette A and click the Go to Link icon at the bottom of the palette B. InDesign instantly highlights the linked object on the screen.

## Reviewing Link Information

Along with the link itself, InDesign stores information about the link and the original graphic file. Select a link and then choose Link Information from the Links palette menu to see where the original file is located, when it was last modified, and what its file type is.

## Relinking Graphics

Because InDesign creates a link to the original file you placed, you can easily replace one linked graphic with another. For example, you may want to work with a low-resolution version of an image for placement purposes, and then replace it with a high-resolution version just before printing. Or you may simply need to repair a link that was broken when you moved an image file. To relink a graphic, select its link in the Links palette, click the Relink icon at the bottom of the palette (or choose Relink from the palette menu), and then select the file you want to link to.

## Updating Links

A symbol **A** appears next to a link in the Links palette if the linked file has been modified. Additionally, InDesign alerts you when you open a document if one or more of your linked graphics have been modified or are missing. To update a link, select the link in the Links palette and click the Update Link icon **B** (or choose Update Link from the palette menu). InDesign automatically updates the link and refreshes the preview in your document.

## Editing Linked Graphic Files

If you've placed a native Illustrator or Photoshop file, you can return to the original application to make quick changes to the file. Select the link in InDesign, and then click the Edit Original icon **A** at the bottom of the palette. InDesign automatically opens the linked file in Illustrator or Photoshop **B**. Just make your changes, save the file, and return to InDesign. It instantly updates the graphic in your document.

## Using File Information

If you've stored file information in Photoshop or Illustrator, it's available to you in InDesign. Select the link, and then choose Link File Info from the Links palette menu. The File Information dialog box includes fields for information about camera settings, credits, and other details you might want to capture about an image or graphic.

# Placing a PDF File

**Place a page from a PDF file as a graphic in your InDesign document.**

### 1. Choose the Place Command.

As with any other graphic, you can import a page from an Adobe PDF file using the Place command. Either choose File > Place, or use the keyboard short-cut (Command-D in Mac OS or Ctrl-D in Windows). InDesign will create a link to any PDF file you import using the Place command. You needn't create or select a frame before placing the file, but if you do, InDesign will automatically place the PDF file in the frame.

### 2. Select the PDF File.

Select the PDF file you want to place, and be sure to select Show Import Options. For this example, we'll place the CD Cover.pdf file.

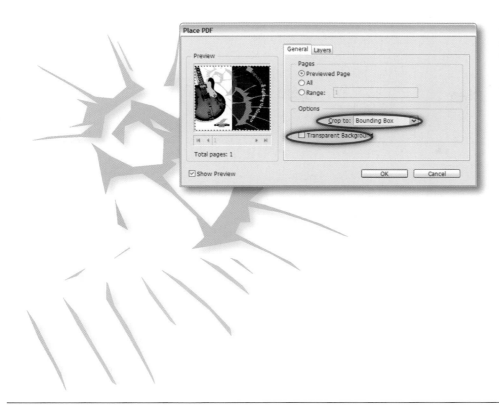

### 3. Select the PDF Page and Crop Options.

The Place PDF dialog box offers different options than the dialog boxes that appear when you import other file formats. PDF files may contain multiple pages, but you can place just one page at a time. Therefore, you'll need to choose which page you want to import. You can scroll through the pages to see a preview of each one if you're not sure. Of course, in our example, there is only one page, so the decision is quite easy.

You can also decide how much of the PDF image to place. You can crop the PDF page using the trim, bleed, or crop lines, or the bounding box.

If you want the PDF file to have a transparent background, select Transparent Background. Here we want the background to be opaque to retain the integrity of the CD case in our advertisement.

Click OK to close the dialog box.

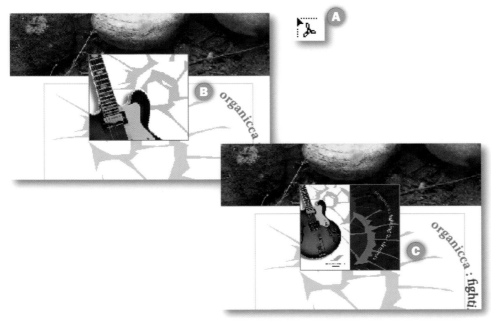

### 4. Place the PDF File in Its Frame.

The cursor changes to a loaded PDF cursor **A**, ready for us to place into an existing frame or just to drop somewhere on the page. Here, we'll place it in this small frame in the center of the ad. This image is way too big for the frame **B**. To scale it proportionally to fit, we'll choose Object > Fitting > Fit Content Proportionally. The keyboard shortcut is Option-Shift-E (Mac OS) or Ctrl-Shift-E (Windows). Now the image fits perfectly into the frame **C**. 🔲

# Working with Native Illustrator and Photoshop Files

One of the great advantages to working in InDesign CS2 is that you can import native Illustrator and Photoshop files. It's much easier to make a quick edit when you're working in the native file format, without having to resave the graphic as a TIFF or EPS file. And InDesign honors transparency in Illustrator and Photoshop files, as well.

## Placing Native Files

You can place a Photoshop (PSD) or Illustrator (AI) file just as you place any other graphic: Choose File > Place and select the file you want to import. Be sure to select Show Import Options so that you can decide what aspects of the file to include and whether to use color management. When you use the Place command to import a native Illustrator or Photoshop file, InDesign creates a link to the original document. The native format for Illustrator CS files is based on Adobe PDF, so the Place PDF dialog box appears when you place a native Illustrator file.

## Dragging and Dropping Files

There's an even quicker way to get native Illustrator and Photoshop files into InDesign, if your import options are already set the way you want them. You can drag and drop a file directly into InDesign from the desktop—either into an existing frame or anywhere on the page. Just as if you'd used the Place command, InDesign creates a link to the original file.

---

**T I P**

**Display Quality.** By default, InDesign displays all images at a normal quality, which may leave some images looking fuzzy **A**. To see a more accurate depiction of how the image will print, Control-click (Mac OS) or right-click (Windows) and then choose Display Performance > High Quality Display **B**. Or select the image and choose View > Display Performance > High Quality Display. InDesign redraws more slowly when it displays images at high quality, particularly large ones, but you get a sharp image **C** when you want one.

## Copying and Pasting Artwork

## Editing Graphics in Illustrator or Photoshop

If you want to include an Illustrator drawing or a Photoshop image in your InDesign document, but you don't need to retain a link to the original, you can copy and paste. Select the part of the document that you want to use in Illustrator or Photoshop, choose Edit > Copy, and then switch to InDesign. Paste the artwork into your InDesign document. The artwork is embedded in the document, but is still editable. For example, you can still change its opacity and resize it. And if it's a vector object, you can edit the individual strokes.

To edit the original graphic in Illustrator or Photoshop, select the link in the Links palette, and then click the Edit Original icon A. Or just press Option (Mac OS) or Alt (Windows) and double-click the file.

InDesign opens the original document in the application you created it in B. You can make any edits you want to make and save the file, and InDesign automatically updates it in your document. 🖏

---

### CAUTION

**Pasting from Illustrator.** Before you copy and paste artwork from Illustrator, make sure that AICB and Preserve Paths are selected in the File Handling and Clipboard pane of the Illustrator Preferences dialog box. It's also best to copy and paste only simple paths, because complex objects pasted into InDesign will no longer be editable.

---

# Photoshop PDF File Format

*Resave a native Photoshop image to preserve the vector data, resulting in a smoother appearance onscreen and in print.*

### 1. Edit the Original Image.

When you import a Photoshop document, even the vector objects in it will print as pixels. When we zoom into this example, we can see the pixelated edges on the shapes and the text. To ensure that the vector objects remain vectors onscreen and when we print the file, we need to save this file from Photoshop in the Photoshop PDF format. And to do that, we need to return to Photoshop. We can get there quickly either by selecting the link to this image and clicking the Edit Original icon in the Links palette or by pressing the Option (Mac OS) or Alt (Windows) key and double-clicking the image. InDesign opens the original image in Photoshop.

## 2. Save as a Photoshop PDF File.

While we're in the Photoshop file, we could make other edits, but in this case, we just want to save the file in the Photoshop PDF format. So we'll choose File > Save As, and then choose the Photoshop PDF format. Be sure to choose the Photoshop PDF format and not the Adobe PDF format, which won't retain Photoshop data.

The Photoshop PDF format retains all of the Photoshop information, including layers, adjustment layers, paths, and so on, so that you can return to Photoshop to edit the file. However, it also lets you retain vector objects and text as vector information.

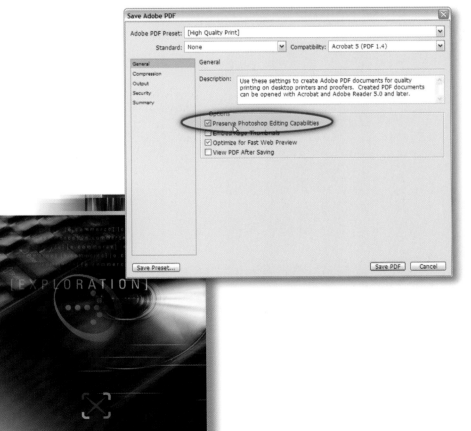

## 3. Set PDF Options.

There are several options you can select when you save a Photoshop PDF file.

Choose a compression option. JPEG compression creates a smaller file but degrades the image each time you compress it. ZIP compression is lossless, so you retain all your image data, but the resulting file is larger. Generally, we recommend using ZIP compression if you're planning to print your document.

Key to our purpose is the preserve Photoshop editing capabilities option. This will allow us to edit the PDF file back in Photoshop.

PDF security is a good idea if you're creating a final document, but not if you're planning to place the file into InDesign or another application. When PDF security is enabled, you cannot place the file.

Click Save PDF to accept the PDF options and save the file.

### 4. Return to InDesign and Relink.

Close Photoshop and return to InDesign. Unlike most times when you use the Edit Original command, InDesign does not automatically update the link, because we've saved the file to a new format, with a new name. We'll need to relink or replace the file. It's probably easiest just to replace it, so choose File > Place, select the new file, select both Show Import Options and Replace Selected Item, and then click Open. Click OK in the Place PDF dialog box because we have just one page in the PDF file. InDesign replaces the original file with the new Photoshop PDF file. When we zoom in, the difference is clear. Vectors are simply smoother and sharper. Even the text looks great.

**Colorize Placed Images.** Don't limit yourself to colorizing grayscale and black-and-white images you've placed into InDesign. With the tricks we share here, you can colorize full-color images you've placed. Or you can convert them to grayscale images.

First, place the image A. We prefer to use PDF files or Photoshop PSD files.

Then, select the image with the Selection tool, copy it to the clipboard, and choose Edit > Paste in Place to paste it directly in front of the original. Next comes the first trick. Using the Direct Selection tool, select the image you pasted and delete it. The frame remains, with the exact size and position of the original image. Select a color in the Swatches palette to apply a

fill to the frame; if you want to create a grayscale image, select either black or white. And now you're ready for the final trick: Open the Transparency palette, and choose Color from the Blending Mode menu B. The underlying image takes on the color of the frame you created C D.

# Using Photoshop Layer Comps

*You can use different layer combinations of a Photoshop image without importing multiple files. Just select the layers or layer comp you want to use.*

## 1. Create the Photoshop File.

Photoshop CS2 lets you create layer comps—sets of layers to create a particular image—within a file, so that you can show alternatives to a client or, as Wayne's done here, create variations of a design for a series of products. It's easy to create a layer comp in Photoshop CS2. Click the Create New Layer Comp icon **A** at the bottom of the Layer Comps palette to capture the current state of layers in the Layers palette.

---

**T I P**

**Quick Switch.** To move quickly from one application to another, press Command-Tab (Mac OS) or Ctrl-Tab (Windows).

## 2. Prepare the InDesign Document.

Let's move over to InDesign. We're creating a set of labels for some organic fruit preserves. Each of the labels will have the same text, so we've added the text files to the master pages and placed the text on a new layer. Then, on page 1, we've created a graphic frame to contain the Photoshop image. We're ready to import the file.

### TIP

**Select It All.** To select every element on a layer, press Option (Mac OS) or Alt (Windows) and select the layer. This is a quick and easy way to verify which elements are on which layers.

## 3. Place the Photoshop file.

There's nothing tricky about placing a Photoshop file with layer comps. Select the graphic frame. Then, just as we've placed other files, we'll choose File > Place. Select the OsborneOrgLabel.psd file. The Status column shows us that the file is open in Photoshop **A**. Make sure Show Import Options is selected, and click Open.

This is where it gets fun. In the Image Import Options dialog box, we can select which layers to include. More important for our project, we can choose which layer comp to use. Select Orange 1 **B**. The orange marmalade label appears in the Preview window. Click OK to import the file. It drops into the graphic frame beautifully **C**.

### 4. Duplicate the page.

We've got one label, but we still need to produce labels for the other flavors of preserves. We'll use a time-saving shortcut to duplicate the page exactly. In the Pages palette, drag the Page 1 icon onto the New Page icon **A**. Page 2 appears in the Pages palette **B**. Turn to page 2 and that's all there is to it. We have an exact duplicate of the first page.

### 5. Choose a different layer comp.

Of course, we don't want every label to be the same. Select the graphic on page 2. Then, choose Object > Object Layer Options. This dialog box looks a lot like the Image Import Options dialog box we used earlier. Here, we can choose a different layer comp without having to import the Photoshop file again. Select the Grape 1 layer comp **A**. If Preview is selected, the Grape label appears on page 2 **B** automatically. Click OK, and we're already done with the second label. Of course, we can do exactly the same thing for the other labels: duplicate the page, select the placed image, choose Object > Object Layer Options, and select a layer comp. It's as easy as pie—or preserves, if you like.

**Changing Dialog Boxes** We're using the Adobe interface for the Place dialog box, because it's consistent between Mac OS and Windows **A**. If you prefer to use the operating system's dialog box, click Use OS Dialog **B**. Most of the functionality is the same, but the Status column is unique to the Adobe interface **C**. Additionally, the Adobe interface provides access to project tools, which are convenient if you're using Version Cue.

# 7

# WORKING WITH TRANSPARENCY

*Adding a Bit of "Wow"*
*to Even the Simplest Page*
*with Drop Shadows,*
*Feathering, and Other*
*Transparency Effects*

W
HEN ADOBE INDESIGN 2.0 introduced support for transparency, it opened a vast new range of graphic options. InDesign CS2 expanded possibilities even further. Sometimes it can be hard to know just where to start—or where to quit. Like investors buying up tech stocks in the late '90s, you can easily end up with too much of a good thing. That is, drop shadows, glows, and various opacity settings can enliven and polish your document, but if you overdo it, you can end up visually bankrupt.

Just as you're careful about the number of fonts on a page or the impact of the colors you use, be selective about how you use transparency effects so that they're tasteful and effective. While there are too many ways to incorporate transparency effects for us to cover them all in detail, we hope this chapter will inspire you to think creatively about how you can manipulate graphics and placed images in InDesign so that you can create your own graphic techniques.

### Transparency

Any Adobe Photoshop user will instantly recognize the blending modes in the Transparency palette. As in Photoshop, blending modes use transparency to blend colors with the colors in the objects beneath them. Additionally, the Transparency palette itself looks very much like the same palette in Adobe Illustrator, with its Opacity slider. On such familiar ground, you'll be able to start creating cool effects quickly.

You can use blending modes and transparency with graphics you create in InDesign as well as those you place.

In fact, InDesign recognizes any transparency present in native Photoshop and Illustrator files you place into InDesign, and you can blend those graphics with other objects on the page. We'll show you the advantages of using native file formats whenever you're placing Photoshop or Illustrator graphics in an InDesign layout.

### Putting It All Together

In this chapter, we use a cool old guitar and a CD label to get some of the InDesign features rockin'. We show you how to use a standard drop shadow—easy to apply in InDesign—and then go one better to create a three-dimensional shadow that you'd usually see in Photo-shop. How do we do it? We use a series of blends, feathering, skewing, multiplying, and fingers-crossing to pull it off.

If you're looking for something simpler, use the drop shadow feature to create a glow around an object. And though we don't really need them anymore, we put the humble clipping path to the test, as well.

### Achieving the Unusual

We know you don't work with InDesign in a vacuum, and it's sometimes more powerful when you pair it with other Adobe applications. So we'll hop in and out of Illustrator to copy and paste some graphics as we create a stylish wine label with an unusual shape.

Documents that stray from the typical rectangle have been difficult to create and challenging to present to clients. Now, using layers and a bit of crafty artwork, you can turn a production artist's worst nightmare into a designer's dream come true.

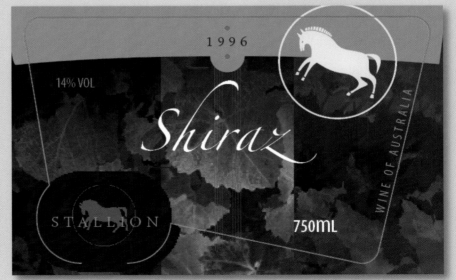

# The Transparency Palette

The most obvious way to use transparency in InDesign is to apply it using the Transparency palette. You can add transparency to almost any object in your document and specify how an object's colors interact with the colors of the objects behind it on the page.

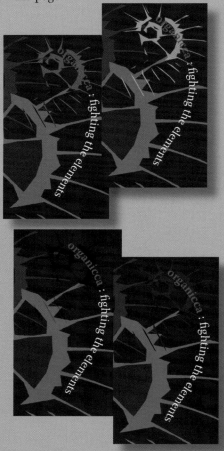

## Opening the Palette

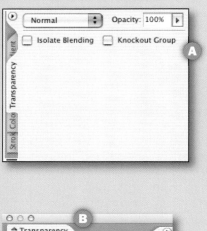

As you probably guessed, you can open the Transparency palette by choosing Window > Transparency. By default, it's docked on the right side of your screen **A**. You might find it easiest to pull the Transparency palette loose so that you can move it around your screen as you work **B**. Because it's a simple palette, it actually takes up less space on the screen when it's undocked.

## Opacity

The Opacity setting determines how opaque an object is, and therefore how transparent it is. You can change the opacity for any object you place in InDesign, even an Adobe PDF file, as well as any object you draw. Type in an Opacity value if you already know how transparent you want an object to be, or use the slider to experiment. As you change the value, InDesign dynamically updates the screen preview.

## *Blending Modes*

If you've used Photoshop, you're probably familiar with blending modes. In both Photoshop and InDesign, blending modes determine how the colors of objects blend with the colors of underlying objects. By default, the blending mode is set to Normal A, which displays the top object without regard to the object below it. You can get some exciting effects using other blending modes, though, and we recommend testing them in your documents. In this case, for example, Luminosity B is interesting, and Color Burn C is good, too.

# Creating a Drop Shadow

*Use the drop shadow feature to instantly create a drop shadow for any object on the page.*

### 1. Select the Object or Objects.

You can apply a drop shadow to one object or to all of the objects in your document. Use the Selection tool to select any object you want to apply a drop shadow to. (Press the Shift key to select more than one object.) Drop shadows are most dramatic on irregular shapes, but they can be effective on any object. Here, we'll apply a drop shadow to this guitar.

### 2. Apply a Drop Shadow.

It really couldn't be easier to apply the drop shadow. Just choose Object > Drop Shadow, and check the Drop Shadow box. Presto. You've got a drop shadow. To see the results in real time, select the Preview option in the Drop Shadow dialog box.

### 3. Modify the Drop Shadow.

When you first apply the drop shadow, InDesign uses the default settings in the Drop Shadow dialog box. You can modify those to make the shadow darker or lighter, change its position, use a different blending mode, or even change the color. Experiment with the options to find the drop shadow that works best for your document.

### 4. Create a Glow Effect with the Drop Shadow.

One of the fun things you can do with the Drop Shadow feature is to create a halo, or glow effect, around an object. To create a halo, change the offset values to 0 so that the shadow is directly below the image. Then increase the opacity to about 89%, and add a blur of about 4 mm so that it shows around all the edges. Now, choose a color for your glow. ▥

# Adding a 3D Shadow

*Create your own 3D shadow when you need a stronger effect than a simple drop shadow provides. All you'll need to get started is an image saved from Photoshop with a clipping path, which essentially crops the image.*

---

**Clipping Path Optional.** In the old days, you needed to create a clipping path in Photoshop to ensure a transparent background in a page-layout application. However, in InDesign CS2, the clipping path isn't necessary. That's because InDesign supports transparency in Photoshop documents. Of course, you can still use the clipping path if you want to: Choose Object > Clipping Path to specify how InDesign recognizes it.

**1. Convert a Clipping Path to a Frame.**
When an object in an InDesign document has a clipping path, you can select it using the Direct Selection tool **A**. A clipping path crops an image so that only a part of it appears through the shape, hiding unwanted parts of the image or providing an irregular border.

Currently, our guitar is in a frame that is the size and shape of its bounding box. We'd like to be able to use the clipping path as a frame. To do that, Control-click (Mac OS) or right-click (Windows), and then choose Convert Clipping Path to Frame from the contextual menu **B**. Now the frame is in the shape of the clipping path.

## 2. Copy the Image.

We're creating a 3D drop shadow for our image, but we want to leave the image itself unchanged. So we need to copy the image now, and the copy is what we'll work with to create the shadow. Choose Edit > Copy, and then Edit > Paste. Now we have two guitars.

## 3. Delete the Copied Image, Leaving the Frame.

This step may seem a little nonintuitive. We want to remove the guitar image itself, leaving only the frame behind. Select the guitar with the Direct Selection tool, and press the Delete key. The guitar is gone; the frame remains. If anything else happens, remember that you can undo it by pressing Command-Z (Mac OS) or Ctrl-Z (Windows) and then try again.

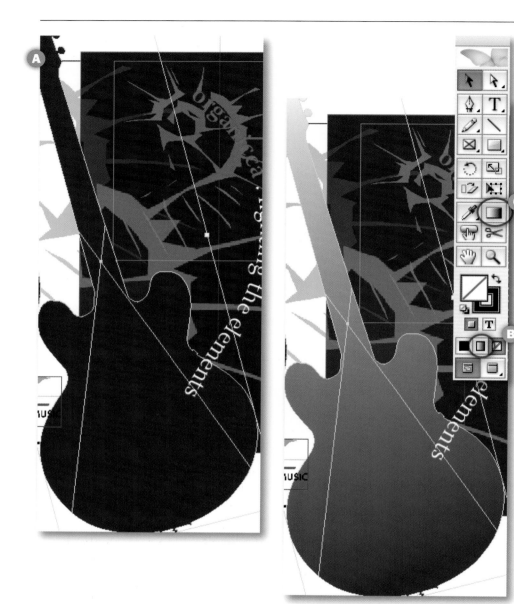

### 4. Fill the Frame.

This is the basic shape for our shadow. Now, a shadow has to have some kind of fill or it's not a very effective shadow. So we'll apply a black fill to this frame. That will give us a solid black silhouette **A**. Most shadows aren't solid black, though, so let's apply a gradient to make this a little more realistic. Click the Apply Gradient icon in the Toolbox **B**. Then, with the Gradient tool **C**, click and drag across the frame to set the direction of the gradient.

## 5. Soften the Edges.

Shadows don't have hard edges, so we need to soften the border on our silhouette by feathering the edges. Feathering works just as it does in Photoshop. Choose Object > Feather. Select the Preview option in the Feather dialog box so that you can see how it looks as you adjust it. You can choose how hard or soft the shadow will be. For this example, we'll type *3 mm* for the feather width. You can also play with the Corners options to see what you like best.

We'd like this shadow to blend into the background a bit, so let's turn to our trusty Transparency palette and change the settings. We'll drop the opacity to 65%. Then choose Multiply, the blending mode of choice for shadows because it darkens everything underneath.

## 6. Position the Shadow.

We have the shadow—now we just need to put it under our guitar. First, move it near the original object **A**. Obviously, a shadow goes behind an object, so let's send it to the back. Choose Object > Arrange > Send to Back, or use the keyboard shortcut: Command-Shift-[ (Mac OS) or Ctrl-Shift-[ (Windows).

Next, we'll distort the shadow to give it a three-dimensional effect. Start by dragging the frame down a bit lower than the original. Then we'll select the top frame handle and squash the frame down **B**. Next, using the Shear tool, let's shear the guitar shadow about 11.7 degrees **C**. Then move the shadow under the guitar again. Nudge it until it meets your satisfaction.

Of course, you'll get different effects with different values. How much you skew the shadow and where you position it depends on the effect you want for the project you're working on. 🔲

# Creating a Vector Mask

*Use a vector mask, which creates a sharp-edged shape on the page, to preview an unusual document edge, such as the one that outlines this wine label, in InDesign.*

### 1. Open the Original Graphic in Illustrator.

To preview this wine label without the distraction of the background, we'll create a vector mask along the die line, the line along which the label will be cut. The die line originated in Illustrator, and we'll need to return to Illustrator to begin to create our vector mask. Select the link in the Links palette and click the Edit Original button. The die line graphic will automatically open in Illustrator.

## 2. Copy the Image and Paste It into InDesign.

We're not actually going to edit this image. Instead, we'll copy it and paste it into our InDesign document. Before we do that, though, we need to make sure the paths will be included. Choose Illustrator > Preferences (Mac OS) or Edit > Preferences (Windows), and then select the File Handling & Clipboard pane. In the Clipboard on Quit section of the pane, select AICB and Preserve Paths. Click OK.

Now we'll select the entire die line, copy it to the clipboard (choose Edit > Copy), and then return to InDesign. There, we'll just paste it (choose Edit > Paste). Now the actual vector shape is in InDesign. If you select it with the Direct Selection tool, you can see the points and paths **A**.

Let's apply a stroke color in InDesign, as well. Magenta will really help distinguish the die line from the rest of the image **B**.

## 3. Replace the Original Die Line.

When we pasted the die line into InDesign, it didn't drop in exactly where the original die line was. Let's drag it into place, so that it is precisely aligned with the die line. After we've positioned the new die line on top of the old one, we'll select the original die line and press Delete. If you have any difficulty selecting the original die line, press Command (Mac OS) or Ctrl (Windows) while you click.

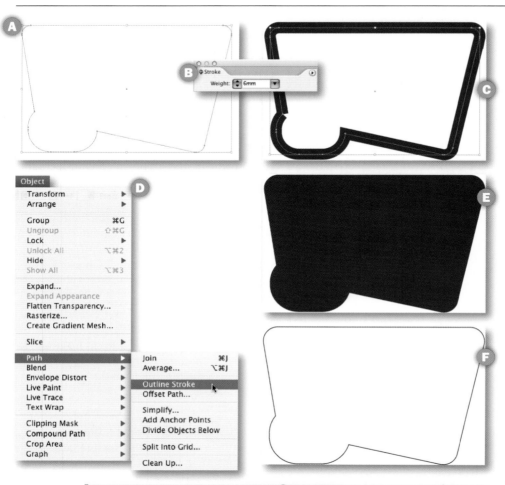

### 4. Create a Bleed Mark Outline in Illustrator.

Because we're using an unusual shape for our wine label, it's difficult to see exactly where the bleed line will be. We'd like to be able to crop the image to the bleed line. Once again, we'll go to Illustrator for a bit of help. The die line document is still open in Illustrator **A**.

We want the bleed mark to be 3 mm outside the trim area. Open the Stroke palette, and set the stroke to 6 mm **B**. This extends the stroke to 3 mm inside the trim and 3 mm outside it **C**. Next, we'll give the outside of the shape its own keyline: Choose Object > Path > Outline Stroke **D**. Now, use the Direct Selection tool to delete the interior line **E**.

We've got our shape, but it has a black fill and no stroke. Switch the fill and stroke colors, so that we're left with just a keyline **F**. Now we're ready to copy it and paste it into InDesign. Then we'll just drag it into position around the die line.

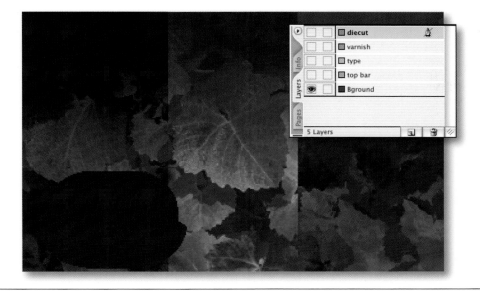

## 5. Copy the Background Elements to the Clipboard.

We've got our bleed line, but the image still extends beyond it. To crop that image to the bleed line, we'll need to do some fancy footwork with layers. We've got several layers, including the die cut, varnish, type, and background. Let's hide everything but the background layer. Then choose Edit > Select All to select everything on the background layer, choose Object > Group to group it, and finally choose Edit > Cut to move it to the clipboard.

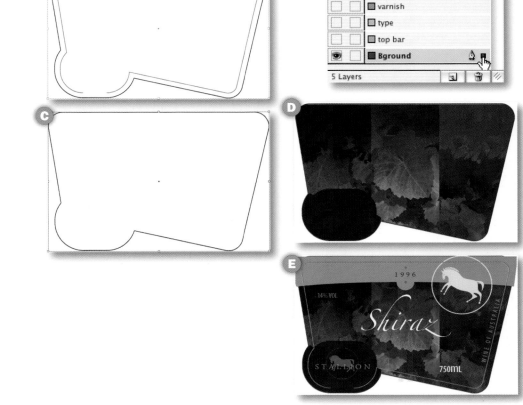

## 6. Paste the Background Elements into the Die Line Area.

Show the diecut layer, and select the bleed line **A**. Then move the bleed area to the Bground layer by clicking the small box to the right side of the diecut layer name and dragging it onto the Bground layer **B**. Hide the diecut layer, so that we're seeing just the Bground layer. All that's on the Bground layer is the bleed line **C**.

Remember that our background objects are on the clipboard, so all we need to do now is choose Edit > Paste Into, and the background images paste into the bleed line **D**. To see the whole label, show all the layers **E**.

### 7. Create a New Layer for the Mask.

We can see just the bleed area, so we're making progress. But we still want to be able to preview the label itself, without the bleed.

First, we'll create a new layer, so that we're not making any permanent changes to our label. Hold down Option (Mac OS) or Alt (Windows) as you click the New Layer button in the Layers palette. In the New Layer dialog box, name the layer "mask."

Now, we'll copy the die line and then paste it in place in the mask layer (choose Edit > Paste In Place). Hide everything else so that we can see clearly what we're doing. All we've got on the mask layer is the die line. Let's give it a fill of hot pink.

### 8. Create the Mask.

We're going to mask the area outside the die line, so that nothing underneath our mask will show. We're going to use the Pathfinder palette to do that. If you're savvy in Illustrator, you probably already know about the Pathfinder palette, as it works the same way in both applications.

Let's just draw a rectangle over the entire page, and give it a black fill, at 100% opacity. Then we'll send it to the back. (Press Command-Shift-[ in Mac OS or Ctrl-Shift-[ in Windows.)

Select both objects and then click the Subtract icon in the Pathfinder palette. The die line shape knocks out of the black rectangle. We have our mask. Now let's show all the other layers, and we can see the complete label against a black background.

**Pathfinder.** The Pathfinder palette lets you create compound shapes from two or more shapes. For example, you can add two individual shapes together to make a single shape. To do that, you'd use the Add icon **A**. When you click the Subtract icon **B**, objects in the front knock out the object at the back (as happened when we created our mask). Intersect **C** is a little more complicated; it creates a shape from the areas of your selected shapes that overlap. Exclude Overlap **D** does the opposite: it creates a shape from the areas that don't overlap. Minus Back **E** reverses the Subtract option; when you use Minus Back, objects in the back knock out the object at the front.

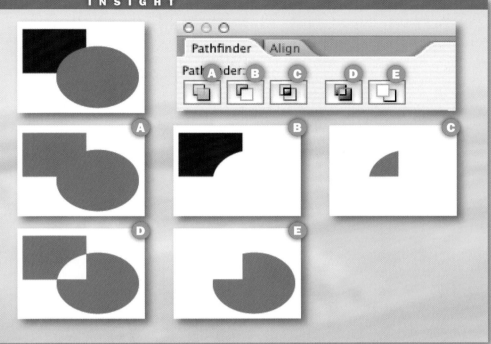

### 9. Change the Background Color and Make It Nonprinting.

We have just a little cleanup work to do. First, let's change the fill on this mask to white, so that we're previewing the label against a white background. Then, because this mask is only for proofing, let's make sure the bleed area prints when we send the job to our professional printer. We'll make the mask nonprinting. Open the Attributes palette by choosing Window > Attributes. Then select the mask and check the Nonprinting box in the Attributes palette. ▥

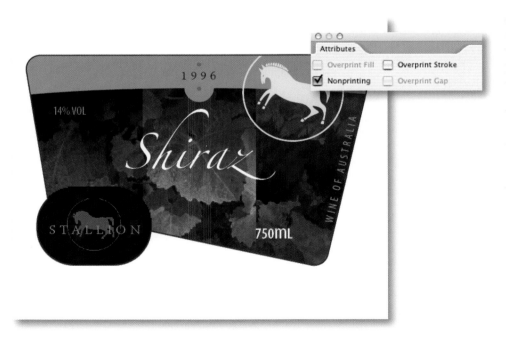

**INSIGHT**

**Noisy Drop Shadows and Feathers.** In InDesign CS2, you can also add noise to a drop shadow or to feathering. Noise gives the effect a grainier texture, and it's a great remedy for banding effects that sometimes crop up in drop shadows. Drag the Noise slider to the right to make the texture rougher or grainier.

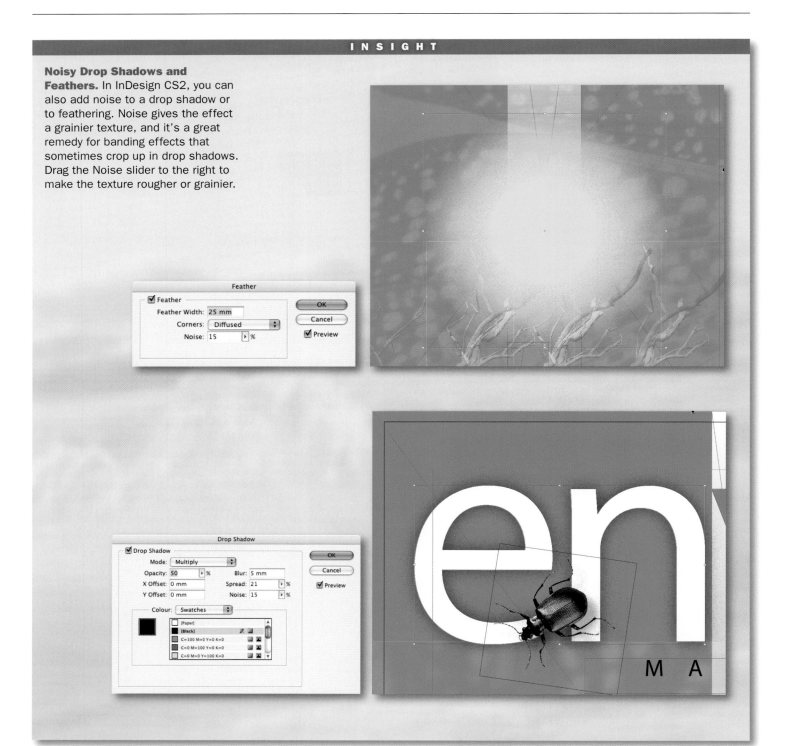

**Spreading Shadows.** You can spread the footprint of your drop shadow, relative to the blur, using the Spread option in InDesign CS2. Move the slider to the right to increase the spread; at 100%, the spread eliminates the blur, resulting in a sharp edge. A spread of 15% spreads the shadow out by 15% of the Blur value. We recommend experimenting with this option to see how it changes the effect. Be sure to select Preview in the dialog box so you can see the results immediately!

**TIP**

**Previewing Drop Shadows** For a more accurate look at how your drop shadows will print, especially if you've applied noise, Control-click (Mac OS) right-click (Windows) or the object, and then choose Display Performance > High Quality Display from the context menu.

| | |
|---|---|
| Cut | ⌘X |
| Copy | ⌘C |
| Paste | ⌘V |
| Paste in Place | ⌥⇧⌘V |
| Zoom | ▶ |
| Transform | ▶ |
| Transform Again | ▶ |
| Arrange | ▶ |
| Select | ▶ |
| Lock Position | ⌘L |
| Stroke Weight | ▶ |
| Content | ▶ |
| Drop Shadow... | ⌥⌘M |
| Feather... | |
| Interactive | ▶ |
| Tag Frame | ▶ |
| Display Performance | ▶ |
| Tag Frame | ▶ |

| |
|---|
| Fast Display |
| Typical Display |
| High Quality Display |
| ✓ Use View Setting |

# ADDING INTERACTIVE ELEMENTS

*Bringing Your Document to Life with Navigational Tools and Hyperlinks*

I F YOU DON'T BLOW your own trumpet, nobody will. This chapter is about showcasing all the great stuff you create in an interactive Adobe PDF folio you export from Adobe InDesign. As soon as the door of opportunity creaks open, email your interactive PDF straight through it and onto the desks of potential clients or employers. They will be so impressed by the convenience that they'll take the time to notice what you have to offer.

Adobe InDesign has become the greatest tool for creating interactive PDF files, bar none. As always, it gives you the page-layout functions of style sheets and master pages, and a huge list of importable graphics (which now even includes movies!). It's also easy to create buttons with rollover states, hyperlinks, and an array of other behaviors—all put to work as soon as you export the document to PDF. In fact, you can author an entire project and export the finished result directly to PDF before you can say, "Holy hyperlink, Batman!"

### All the Benefits of Print, Plus More

We think most people have figured out that exporting HTML code from a page-layout application really isn't the way to go. Page-layout applications such as InDesign give you the maximum flexibility for creating printed documents—and that flexibility simply isn't as possible with HTML. Whether you want to post your document on the Web, distribute it for review, or email it to readers, PDF files are handy. They provide a compact electronic version of the document without sacrificing the integrity of the design. And InDesign makes it easy to export PDF files successfully.

[PACKAGING]

STUDIO 2004

**Packaging** > New release CD for the very popular New Age Group: Organicca.

GOODEARTHMUSIC

With few exceptions, you can embed fonts as you export the PDF from InDesign, avoiding font-substitution issues. You can also embed multiple formats of graphics, so that you can use the same source file to create a high-resolution version of a document to print and a low-resolution version to post on a Web site or distribute through email. InDesign also gives you access to sophisticated security options that ensure that only authorized people can make changes or copy the materials—or, if you prefer, you can even prevent anyone from opening the file without a password.

Designing a PDF file in InDesign opens possibilities beyond those you have when you create for print. For example, you can give your viewers navigational elements such as buttons and bookmarks. You can include motion graphics, video clips, and sound. You can even hide fields until the reader moves the pointer over a certain area.

### Make It Yours

Next time you're preparing a presentation, put the Microsoft PowerPoint away and get out InDesign. You'll have all the flexibility you need to create just the presentation you want, using existing PDF files, Adobe Photoshop images, Adobe Illustrator artwork, and other objects as you wish. Export the interactive PDF file, and use Adobe Acrobat in full-screen mode to show it off.

With a little creative interpretation, you can use these techniques to create a whole host of documents. Think of the possibilities: interactive stationery, secure exams, interactive price lists, books, and, of course, a portfolio to show off your interactive documents!

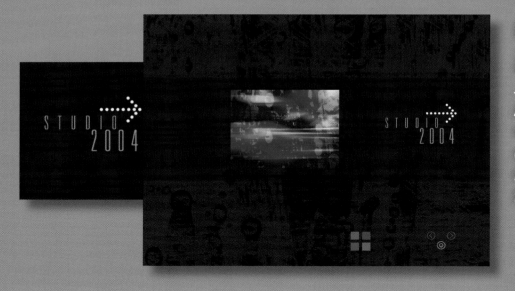

# Creating Hyperlinks

*Add hyperlinks to help viewers move to another destination quickly within an interactive PDF file exported from InDesign CS2.*

## 1. Select the Object You Want to Use as a Link.

We've all become used to the convenience of hyperlinks on the Web, and we've come to expect them everywhere. Fortunately, it's easy to create hyperlinks in InDesign, so that when we convert our document to an interactive PDF file, readers can navigate it efficiently. You can create hyperlinks from text or graphics. Start by selecting the object or section of text you want to use as a hyperlink. In our example, we'll use an imported Illustrator graphic on the first page.

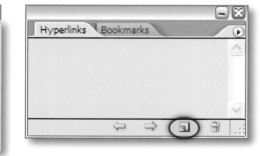

**T I P**

**Hyperlinks to URLs.** If you're linking to a URL that you've listed in the text, you can save a little time creating the hyperlink. Just select the URL text with the Type tool, and then choose New Hyperlink from URL in the Hyperlinks palette. InDesign automatically fills in the URL for you.

## 2. Create a New Hyperlink.

InDesign has a Hyperlinks palette, so you can work with hyperlinks the way you work with links, layers, and many other features. Open the Hyperlinks palette by choosing Window > Interactive > Hyperlinks. Then click the New Hyperlink icon at the bottom of the palette, or choose New Hyperlink from the Hyperlinks palette menu.

### 3. Specify the Destination for the Hyperlink.

In the New Hyperlink dialog box, name the link and choose a destination. If you're linking to another page in the document, choose Page from the Type menu **A**, and then type a page number and choose a zoom setting. If you're linking to a different document, browse to find the document you're linking to. In our example, we'll link to page 2.

If you're linking to a Web site, choose URL from the Type menu **B**. Then type the Web-site address in the URL field, and name the URL if you want to.

If you want to link to specific text in the document, choose Text Anchor from the Type menu **C**, and then choose the text anchor by name. To choose a text anchor, you must first have created one as a hyperlink destination. (See "Defining Destinations" on this page.)

### 4. Specify the Hyperlink Appearance.

Depending on the type of document you're creating, you may want to make hyperlinks obvious on the page, or you may rely on context to help readers find them. Choose whether to make the hyperlink a visible or an invisible rectangle. If you choose to make it visible, choose the color, width, and style for the stroke. You can also choose how it will appear when it's highlighted (inverted, outlined, inset, or normal).

We're going to use an invisible rectangle because our graphic already makes it obvious that this is a hyperlink. Then we'll click OK to close the dialog box. Now the graphic is a link. When readers click it in the PDF file, they'll jump straight to page 2. 〓

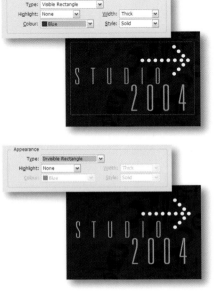

# Creating Buttons

*Convert any object in InDesign into a button with different appearances for different states.*

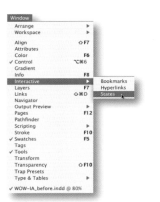

## 1. Open the States Palette.

Buttons can change appearance, depending on the position or action of the reader's pointer. For example, a button might be highlighted in a rollover state, which occurs when the pointer rolls over the button. Or it may change color when someone clicks on it. Each of those conditions is called a *state*. To work with button states in InDesign, open the States palette. Choose Window > Interactive > States.

## 2. Convert an Object to a Button.

Select the object you want to convert into a button. You can select an imported graphic, an object you drew in InDesign, or a text frame. Then choose Object > Interactive > Convert to Button. If you're in Normal View mode, InDesign identifies the button on the screen **A**. Additionally, the States palette becomes active and has one state in it **B**.

In our document, we'll convert one of these navigational icons into a button. Three have already been converted to buttons; we'll convert the fourth.

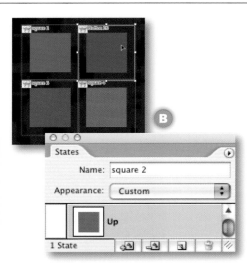

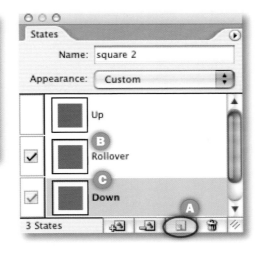

### 3. Create a New State for the Button.

When you first create a button, the States palette contains only the Up state. The Up state is the default state for a button, when the mouse isn't interacting with it at all. In order to change its appearance, we'll need to create another state. Click the New Optional State icon **A**. InDesign adds a Rollover state **B** to the palette. If you click the New Optional State icon again, InDesign adds a Down state **C** to the palette.

Give the button a name you'll remember, and then press Return or Enter. (If you forget to press Return or Enter, the button name will return to its default of Button 1, Button 27, or the like.)

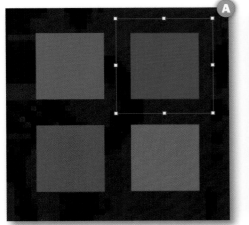

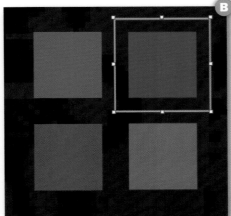

### 4. Change the Appearance for Different States.

Initially, each state is identical, but there isn't much point in having different states if the button doesn't change. So this is our opportunity to change the appearance for each state. Select the state you want to edit, and then make changes to the button.

For our button, let's select the Up state. Then, use the Direct Selection tool to select the orange border. Click the Apply None button in the Toolbox so that the border disappears. When the pointer isn't over the button, it will appear without a border **A**; when the pointer rolls over the button, the border appears **B**.

To see how your button appears in different states, select it with the Selection tool, and then click each state in the States palette. ▥

# Adding Behaviors to Buttons

Link to a URL, show or hide a field, play a movie, or go to a different page using a button. You can assign behaviors to buttons based on mouse events, such as when the pointer enters or exits the button area. To add a behavior, select the button and then choose Button Options from the States palette menu. Select the Behaviors tab.

## Events

The mouse event triggers the behavior you set. Some of the event names are intuitive; others are a little less clear. Mouse Up occurs when the mouse button is released after a click. Mouse Down occurs when the mouse button is initially clicked. Mouse Enter is when the pointer enters the button area; Mouse Exit is when it leaves. On Focus takes effect when the button is highlighted (such as when someone tabs to it); On Blur happens when the focus changes to a different button or field.

## Closing the Document

If you want the PDF document to close when an event occurs, choose Close; if you want to completely exit the application in which the PDF document is open (usually Adobe Reader), choose Exit.

## Going Places

You can use a button to send a reader to another page, a specific anchor or bookmark, or a URL. Or, you can send readers back or forward along their path through the document. Choose Go To Anchor to jump to a bookmark or hyperlink anchor you've created. Choose Go To First Page, Go To Last Page, Go To Next Page, or Go To Previous Page to send a reader to one of those pages. Choose Go To Previous View to send readers to the page they most recently viewed; choose Go To Next View to jump forward after moving backward. (These behaviors work like the Back and Forward buttons in a Web browser.) Choose Go To URL to send the reader to a Web site.

## Multimedia

You can use a button to play a movie or a sound clip in an interactive PDF document. Choose Movie to play, pause, stop, or resume a selected movie. Choose Sound to play, pause, stop, or resume the selected sound clip. (Only movies and sound clips that have been added to the document are available for selection, so you must add the clip to the document before assigning behaviors to buttons for it.)

## Open a File

You can use a button to open another file, which can be a PDF document or any other file. Remember, though, that the reader needs to have an application that can support the file type in order to open it successfully. Also, you'll need to specify an absolute pathname, such as c:\docs\sample.pdf. This option is often most useful if you're creating a document that will accompany others on a CD.

**T I P**

**Convert to PDF.** When you use the Open File behavior, your reader needs to have an application installed that can open the file. It may be simpler to convert the file to PDF so that you know all readers can view it.

## Show or Hide Fields

Sometimes you want a field to appear only when the reader has selected a particular button. For example, you might want additional text to appear, explaining an option. You can use the Show/Hide Fields option to reveal or hide fields depending on the reader's behavior. It's a great way to reduce clutter on the page.

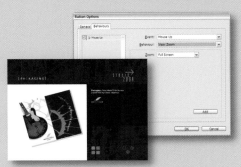

## Change the Zoom Level

If you're displaying a map or a piece of artwork, you might want to make it very easy for your readers to zoom in. Use the View Zoom behavior to display the page according to the zoom level, page layout, and orientation you specify. ▥

# Placing a Graphic for a Button State

**Use a different image to show that a button state has changed.**

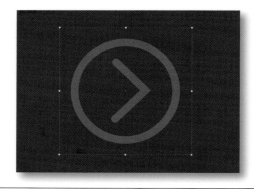

### 1. Convert an Object into a Button.

Select the object you want to use as a button, and then choose Object > Interactive > Convert to Button. In our example, we're using an Illustrator file called Next.ai to create a Next button on the master page. The Next.ai file will be the default appearance for the button, assigned to the Up state. Open the States palette and choose Window > Interactive > States.

### 2. Create a Rollover State.

We'd like this graphic to look different when the pointer rolls over it. Let's create a Rollover state by clicking the New Optional State icon. InDesign adds a rollover state to the States palette.

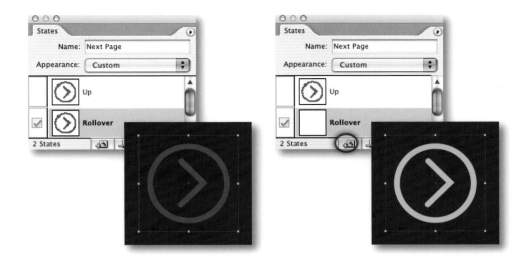

### 3. Place a Graphic into the State.

Now, we want the rollover state to use a different graphic. Click the Place Content into Selected State icon at the bottom of the palette. Then select the graphic to use. You can use an Illustrator file, a Photoshop file, or any other graphic file. We're using an Illustrator file named Next_o.ai. This file is exactly the same as the Next.ai file, except it's white. Select Open to bring the file in. InDesign places it in the original graphic's spot, and it's assigned to the rollover state.

We'll name this button *Next Page*, and press Return or Enter.

### 4. Assign Behaviors to the States.

Anyone clicking the Next Page button will expect to go to the next page, so we'd better set it up that way. Choose Button Options from the States palette menu, and then click the Behaviors tab in the Button Options dialog box. Choose an event and a behavior. We're choosing Mouse Up for the event, so the behavior will occur when the mouse button is released after clicking. And because this is the Next Page button, we'll choose Go To Next Page for the behavior. Click Add, and then click OK. 🎞

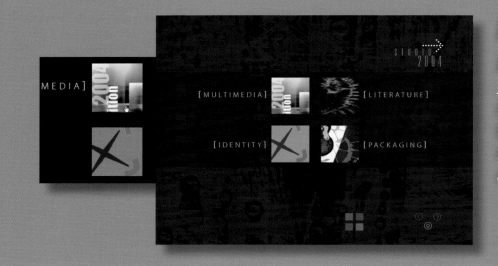

# Displaying Hidden Fields

*Use a button's behavior to display a field, such as informational text, when it's appropriate.*

### 1. Create the Contextual Button.

We'd like our readers to see the text that explains the button when they mouse over it. For example, when the pointer rolls over the PACKAGING button, the word *Packaging* should appear next to it. To start, then, we need to convert the *Packaging* text to a button. Select the text frame with the Selection tool, and choose Object > Interactive > Convert to Button.

**T I P**

**It Won't Go Away.** Don't let it worry you that you can still see the button in InDesign. It will become invisible when we create the PDF. Until then, you need to be able to see it InDesign to edit it or move it as you design your document.

### 2. Make the Button Invisible.

By default, this button should be invisible. We only want it to show when someone moves the pointer over the graphic next to it. So, choose Button Options from the States palette menu. In the General pane, choose Hidden from the Visibility in PDF menu. While we're in the Button Options dialog box, let's name the button *Packaging Text*. Click OK.

### 3. Create the Trigger Button.

We have a hidden button now, but we need to create the button that will reveal it. As always, you can create a button from any graphic, drawn object, or text frame. We'll draw a rectangle over the graphic in our document, with no fill or stroke. Then choose Object > Interactive > Convert to Button.

### 4. Assign the Behavior to Show the Field.

This is the button that does all the heavy lifting to show the text button we created earlier. Choose Button Options from the States palette menu. Name the button *Packaging button*, and then click the Behaviors tab. Choose Mouse Enter for the event, because we want the behavior to occur whenever the mouse pointer enters the button area. Then choose Show/Hide Fields from the Behavior menu.

All the fields in the document are listed here. This is where you really appreciate having good names for your fields. Click next to the field you want to show; an eye icon appears next to it. We'll click next to Packaging Text. This means that the field we named Packaging Text will show when the pointer enters the button area. Click Add. Now we've accomplished the first half of this task.

### 5. Assign the Behavior to Hide the Field Again.

This part can be a little more confusing, so be sure to try it a few times. We've arranged to show the text when the pointer enters the button area, but then we need to hide it again when the pointer leaves. Otherwise, we'll have random bits of text left over on the screen; instead of guiding our readers, we could confuse them.

Choose Mouse Exit from the Event menu because we want to hide the text when the pointer leaves the button area. Click next to the field we want to hide until the eye appears, and then click next to it again. You'll see a small red line through the eye. That means the field will hide when the pointer exits the button area. Click Add to make sure the behavior is assigned and then click OK to exit the dialog box. ▥

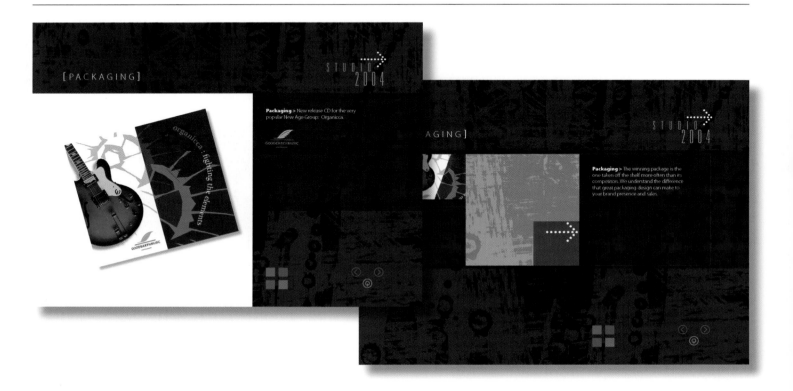

# Planning an Interactive Folio

One of the most important tasks in developing an interactive folio is planning. Before you begin to lay out the pages, first decide which work to present and how you want to group it.

For example, you may choose to group projects in your folio by date, discipline, category, medium, client, or industry. Group your work in the way that best communicates your expertise to your audience.

Be selective. Many people do not have the time to navigate through hundreds of projects. You'll see better results if you keep the presentation simple and to the point.

Keep in mind, as well, that it is *quality* rather than quantity that will grab the viewer's attention.

## Creating a Site Map

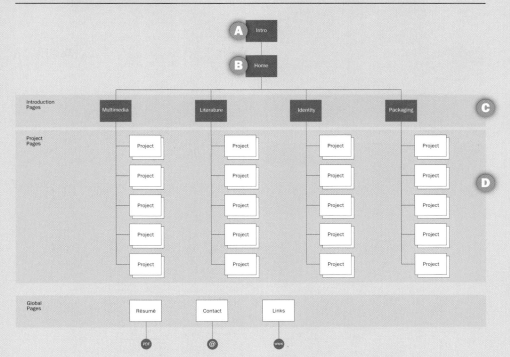

It's easier to compose an interactive document if you first map out the elements as you would for a Web site. A good site map should illustrate three important elements:

*Grouping:* How projects are organized.

*Hierarchy:* Where each piece of information falls within the interactive document.

*Connections:* Where links are placed to allow viewers to jump to other points in the document, to external documents, or to Web sites.

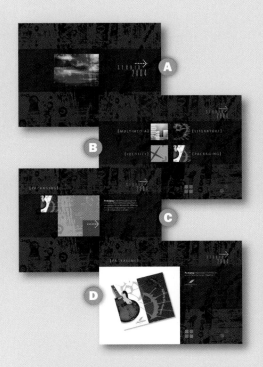

# Adding a Movie

You can add a video clip or movie to your document, and you determine how much control the viewer has. Set the movie to run automatically, to loop, or to play once and stop. Or give your viewers controls to play, pause, and stop the movie whenever they like.

## Placing a Movie

You place a movie in an InDesign document just the way you'd place any other file. Choose File > Place, and then select the movie file you want to include. You can place a QuickTime, AVI, MPEG, or SWF movie. (QuickTime 6.0 is required to work with movies in InDesign.) Click where you want the movie to appear. If you drag the loaded icon to create a media frame, the movie boundary may appear skewed.

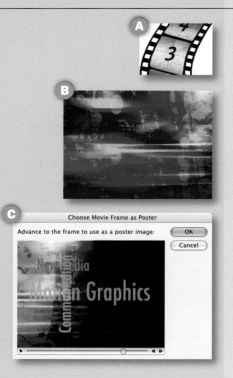

Choose Movie Frame as Poster

Advance to the frame to use as a poster image:     OK     Cancel

## Designate a Poster

The poster is the image that appears in the media frame when the movie isn't playing. To select the poster image, choose Object > Interactive > Movie Options. Then choose one of the following options for the poster: None displays no poster; Standard displays a generic movie poster that has no relationship to the movie itself **A**; Default Poster displays either the poster image packaged with the movie file or, if there is no designated poster image, the first frame of the movie **B**; Choose Image as Poster lets you select an image—click Browse and then select any bitmap graphic you want to use; Choose Movie Frame as Poster lets you select any frame in the video to use as the poster **C**.

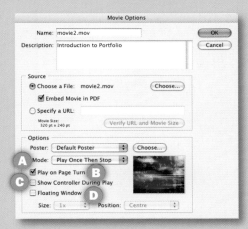

## Determining When the Movie Plays

You can set a movie to play automatically when a viewer turns to that page in the PDF file, or you can provide controls that allow the viewer to play the movie at will. Choose Object > Interactive > Movie Options to control when the movie plays. The Mode setting **A** determines whether the movie plays in a loop. Select Play on Page Turn to play the movie when someone turns to the page it's on **B**. Select Show Controller During Play to give your viewer control over pausing, starting, and stopping the movie **C**. Select Floating Window if you want the movie to play in a separate window **D**.

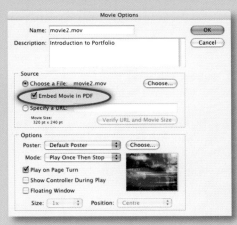

## Embedding a Movie

When you first place a movie file, InDesign links to the file, and it includes that link when you export a PDF. However, you can embed the movie in the PDF document, so that you don't need to provide the movie file separately. Of course, when you embed the movie file, the PDF document is much larger. To embed the movie, select Embed Movie in PDF. (Viewers must use Acrobat 6.x or Adobe Reader 6.x to view an embedded movie.)

### INSIGHT

**Embedded Movies Aren't Compressed.** There are good reasons to embed a movie in a PDF document, but compression isn't one of them. Embedded movies aren't compressed when you export an InDesign document to a PDF file. So if your movie is 100 MB, the PDF document containing it will be at least 100 MB.

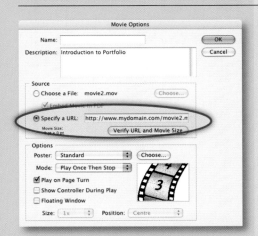

## Streaming a Movie from a Web Site

You can include a movie in your PDF document without embedding it or providing the movie file separately if you stream it from a Web site. To link to a streaming video, select Specify a URL in the Movie Options dialog box, and then enter the URL. To ensure that the URL is valid, click Verify URL and Movie Size. Viewers will be able to stream the video in your PDF file as long as they have an Internet connection.

# Creating an Interactive PDF File

*Export your InDesign document to PDF and see your interactive features in action.*

### 1. Export the File.

When you're ready to test your interactive elements, export the document to PDF. Choose File > Export. Then choose Adobe PDF for the format, and select a location on your hard drive to save the file. Click Save.

**TIP**

**PDF Presets.** If you use the same settings to create PDF files for a particular client or project type, create PDF presets. Then you can go directly to the Export PDF Options dialog box, and all the options will be already in place. Just choose File > PDF Export Presets, and choose the preset you want to use. You can also choose a preset when you're in the Export PDF dialog box.

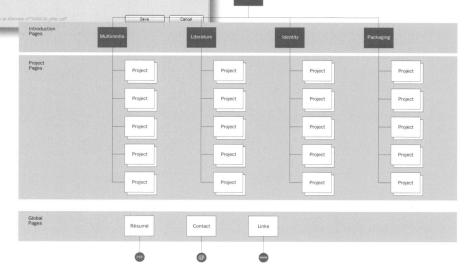

## Export Adobe PDF

Adobe PDF Pre**s**et: [High Quality Print] (modified)

Standard: None    Compatibility: Acrobat 6 (PDF 1.5)

General
Compression
Marks and Bleeds
Output
Advanced
Security
Summary

**General**

Description: [Based on '[High Quality Print]'] Use these settings to create Adobe PDF documents for quality printing on desktop printers and proofers.  Created PDF documents can be opened with Acrobat and Adobe Reader 5.0 and later.

**Pages**
- ⦿ All
- ◯ Range: 1-4
- ☐ Spreads

**Options**
- ☐ Embed Page Thumbnails
- ☑ Optimise for Fast Web View
- ☑ Create Tagged PDF
- ☐ View PDF after Exporting
- ☐ Create Acrobat Layers

**Include**
- ☑ Bookmarks
- ☑ Hyperlinks
- ☑ Visible Guides and Baseline Grid
- ☑ Non-Printing Objects
- ☑ Interactive Elements

Multimedia: Use Object Settings

Save Preset...    Export    Cancel

## 2. Choose PDF Options.

The PDF options you choose depend on how you plan to use the document. If you're printing the document, for example, you'll want to use a higher resolution for images than if you expect the PDF file to be viewed online. However, there are a few settings you should always use when you're including interactive elements such as buttons and movies.

To simplify things, you can use the Acrobat 6 Layered preset, which contains most of the settings that are likely to be appropriate for an interactive PDF file. Most important, though, select Hyperlinks and Interactive Elements from the Include section of the dialog box. And for multimedia, choose Use Object Settings. You can select other options if you need them for your PDF file, but these are the ones that are imperative for an interactive PDF file.

## 3. Test the Document in Acrobat.

All of the interactive elements we've put into our document have been intended for this PDF file, so this is where we really see what we've got. Open the PDF document in Acrobat 6 or later, or in Adobe Reader. Then, test the buttons you've created, and turn to pages that contain multimedia effects. In our case, the PDF file opens to page 1 and the movie automatically plays. When we roll the pointer over a button at the bottom of the page, the border appears. When we click the Next button, its icon changes and we go to the next page. And as we move our pointer over the graphic, *PACKAGING* appears next to it. ▣

**9**

# OUTPUT

*Preparing Your Masterpiece for Perfect Printing or PDF—and Avoiding the Pitfalls*

 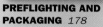

**Y**OU'VE TRAINED HARD and are in great shape. When the starter's gun sounded, you learned your way around the InDesign interface. Continuing on, you aced text and typography, swooped through color, and mastered placed graphics and interactive PDF files. There's just one last high hurdle to cover—printing. Have no fear. Stay with us, and you'll deliver that job in record time.

Whether you are printing a document yourself, sending a file out for commercial printing, or creating a PDF file for clients, this chapter is designed to show you the best way. We'll cover some of the common pitfalls, such as issues concerning transparency and spot colors, and we'll help you develop good habits that will keep you in top form.

### Use the Tools

Before printing or exporting to PDF, make use of InDesign's array of tools to check your files thoroughly. Use the Separations Preview palette we showed

you in Chapter 5 to verify that files separate properly, with everything landing on the appropriate plate. Use the Transparency Flattener Preview palette to see where transparency comes into play and to identify any changes you might want to make to help it all print smoothly. Preflight the document to ensure that the linked files and fonts you used are

all in good shape; then check the details such as graphics' color spaces.

### Think Ahead

InDesign CS2 includes some great tools. Transparency, in particular, offers some amazing effects, but it also requires you to think through the printing process. For example, drop shadows need to be rasterized at output into pixels; how that rasterization occurs depends on the flattener preset you choose in the Print or Export PDF dialog box.

In this chapter, we walk you through these considerations. Take the time to learn where things can go wrong, and take note of the simple steps you can take to ensure success. If you construct your documents with care, you will overcome all obstacles to achieve great output success. You may even feel that you have an unfair advantage after reading this performance-enhancing chapter. It'll be nothing but gold medals for you and InDesign. (Cue the national anthem.)

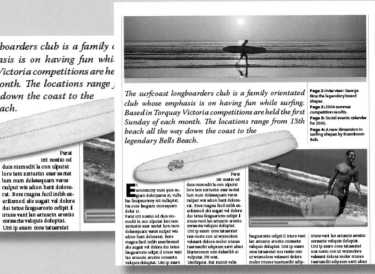

# Preparing Transparent Artwork for Output

Some of the neatest effects you can create in InDesign CS2 are possible due to its support of transparency. To ensure that what you've created onscreen translates well in print, you need to understand how InDesign flattens transparency—and how you can prepare your document for the best results.

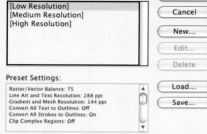

## Understanding the Transparency Flattener

To print correctly, all transparent objects in a file must be flattened. Flattening converts objects with live transparency into visually equivalent opaque objects. To do this, the flattener may need to convert vectors to rasterized areas or type to outlines. How much artwork is rasterized depends on the flattener style you choose. When you use the High Resolution flattener style, more of the original data remains in vector format, typically providing better results.

> **INSIGHT**
>
> **Recognizing Transparency.** You know you're using transparency when you change the opacity using the Transparency palette. However, you're also applying a transparency effect when you create a drop shadow, feather an edge, or import a file from Adobe Photoshop or Adobe Illustrator that uses transparency.

Additionally, the flattener style used during flattening controls the resolution the flattener uses to rasterize transparent areas during flattening. If you're printing to a high-resolution device, be sure to use the High Resolution flattener style so that effects are rasterized at a resolution of 300 dpi. To view preset settings or create custom presets, choose Edit > Transparency Flattener Presets.

## Previewing Transparency

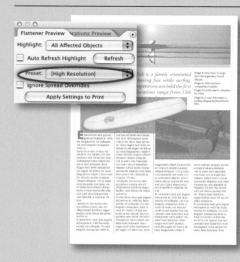

To ensure that you'll get what you expect when you print an InDesign document that includes transparency, preview it onscreen. Choose Window > Output Preview > Flattener to open the Flattener Preview palette. Choose an option from the Highlight menu to see how flattening affects specific parts of your document; choose All Affected Objects to see everything that transparency affects. InDesign highlights the affected areas on the screen. In this example, the drop shadow for the surfboard will be affected, as will some text, the drop cap, and two of the vertical lines. To see just the text that will be outlined, choose Outlined Text from the Highlight menu.

Be sure to choose [High Resolution] from the Preset menu to ensure that InDesign is displaying an accurate preview for settings you'll use when printing.

## Changing the Stacking Order

Because the transparency flattener affects everything that is transparent or that interacts with transparency, the stacking order of your objects becomes very important. If a transparent object is at the top of the stacking order, everything beneath it will be affected by the transparency flattener. However, if it's at the back of the stacking order, objects above it are unaffected.

This is especially critical when you consider text. If text interacts with transparency, it is usually converted to outlines by the flattener. Outlined text looks thicker than text that remains in its original form; having some text outlined and other text normal on a page can be distracting and aesthetically displeasing.

To control which objects are affected by the flattener, change the stacking order. Make sure that text is always at the top of the stacking order, and move your transparent objects as far down in the stacking order as possible. To ensure that text is at the top of the stacking order, you can create a layer just for the text in your document, and then make sure that layer is listed first in the Layers palette.

## Assigning a Transparency Blend Space

When InDesign blends object colors to accommodate transparency, it must blend them into either the CMYK or RGB image space. Choose Edit > Transparency Blend Space > Document CMYK to ensure that transparency effects are blended into the CMYK color space for printed output. If you're creating an online document, you'd probably choose Edit > Transparency Blend Space > Document RGB.

To produce smoother results, it's best to begin with all images in the same color space. If you're working in a CMYK document, convert your images to CMYK before placing them in InDesign.

# Preflighting and Packaging

*Preflight your document to check on linked graphics, fonts, and image specs to avoid time-consuming, expensive errors. Then, package the document and all required files to deliver them efficiently to a service provider or to create a tidy archive.*

### INSIGHT

**RGB Images.** Even when all of your linked images are present, without modifications, InDesign will alert you if any of them use the RGB color space. If you're preparing your document for online distribution, such as a PDF, RGB images are fine. However, if you're planning to print color separations for use on a printing press, heed the alert and convert the images to CMYK using the appropriate CMYK profile before printing.

### 1. Choose File > Preflight.

When you think your document is ready to go, choose File > Preflight. InDesign opens the Preflight dialog box, which displays a summary of all the possible problems in your document. A yellow flag means the issue may or may not be a problem, depending on your workflow. For example, your document may include RGB images, which are fine for online documents but not for high-quality printing. A red flag means the issue is almost certainly a problem, such as a missing link or an incomplete font.

## Preflight (dialog — Fonts pane)

Preflight

| Summary | Fonts |
| Fonts | |
| Links and Images | ⚠ 5 Fonts Used, 1 Missing, 0 Embedded, 0 Incomplete , 0 Protected |
| Colours and Inks | |
| Print Settings | |
| External Plug-ins | |

| Name | Type | Status | Protected |
| --- | --- | --- | --- |
| Myriad Pro S...ld Condensed | OpenType Type 1 | OK | No |
| Warnock Pro Light Caption | OpenType Type 1 | OK | No |
| Warnock Pro Regular | OpenType Type 1 | OK | No |
| Zapfino  Regular | ??? | Missing | ??? |

Current Font

Filename: C:\Program Files\Common Files\Adobe\Fonts\MyriadPro-...

Full Name: Myriad Pro Condensed

First Used: On Page 1

☐ Show Problems Only       Find Font...

Package...   Report...   Cancel

## 2. Verify That Your Fonts Are All Available.

You've carefully selected the appropriate fonts for your document, so you want to ensure that they'll print as you expect. Select the Fonts pane in the Preflight dialog box. InDesign lists all the fonts used in the document, including those embedded in imported graphics, such as PDF or EPS files. It also lists the status of each font, the type of font, and whether it's protected. (Protected fonts cannot be embedded in Adobe PDF or EPS files due to license restrictions.)

If you've used many fonts in the document, you may find it easier to see only the problems. To see only missing, incomplete, and protected fonts, select Show Problems Only.

To correct errors, either install missing fonts on your computer, or click Find Font in the Preflight dialog box and then search for, list, and replace the problematic fonts in your document.

## Preflight (dialog — Links and Images pane)

Preflight

| Summary | Links and Images |
| Fonts | |
| **Links and Images** | ⚠ 0 Links Found: 0 Modified, 0 Missing |
| Colours and Inks | Images: 5 Embedded, 3 use RGB colour space |
| Print Settings | |
| External Plug-ins | |

| Name | Type | Page | Status | ICCProfile |
| --- | --- | --- | --- | --- |
| (Embedded) | RGB | 1 | Embedded | Embedded |
| (Embedded) | PDF | 1 | Embedded | None |
| (Embedded) | PDF | 1 | Embedded | None |
| (Embedded) | RGB | 1 | Embedded | Embedded |

Current Link/Image

Filename: (Embedded)       Update
Link Updated: NA
File Last Modified: NA
Actual ppi: 150x150       Effective ppi: 150x150
Layer Overrides: No
Complete Name: NA

☐ Show Problems Only       Repair All

Package...   Report...   Cancel

## 3. Confirm That Graphics Are Ready for Output.

Depending on the type of graphics you use, there are several things you might want to verify before committing the document for print. Select the Links and Images pane in the Preflight dialog box to see comprehensive information about the placed graphics in the document.

InDesign lists each file, its type, the page number on which it's used, its link status, and whether an ICC profile is embedded. Additionally, when you select a filename, you can see its actual resolution and its effective resolution in pixels per inch. If you've scaled the image, the effective resolution will be different from the original. For best results with high-end printing, images should have an effective resolution of 300 ppi.

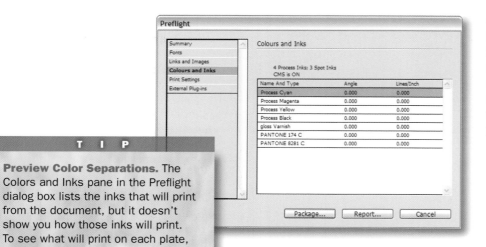

### 4. Check the Inks That Are Used.

If you're printing color separations, verify that you'll be getting the plates you expect. Select the Colors and Inks pane of the Preflight dialog box. InDesign lists each ink. It also checks for spot colors with duplicate definitions, which would print an extra plate.

### 5. Verify the Print Settings, if Appropriate.

When it preflights the document, InDesign checks the current print settings. If you've selected a print preset or specified print settings, verify that they match your requirements. Select the Print Settings pane to see the current settings.

**Printing Instructions**

Filename: Instructions.txt

Contact: Hugh Saturation

Company: Phil Opacity Design

Address: 123 Any Street

Creative Suite 210

Any town

Victoria

Phone: 123-1111 - 1111    Fax: 123-1111 - 1111

Email: Hughsaturation@PhilOpacityDesign.com.au

Instructions: ::NOTE:: We have used Magenta to create the die line spot color.

The job also includes a spot varnish plate

please call with any questions.

Continue

Cancel

**T I P**

**Sticky Information.** It may seem like a bother to type your name, company name, and contact information in the Printing Instructions dialog box, but once you've entered that information, it will automatically come up every time you package an InDesign file.

1996

14% VOL

*Shiraz*

WINE OF AUSTRALIA

STALLION

750ML

### 6. Package the Files.

Once you've ensured that all is well with your document, you can bundle all the files required to print it into a folder. Send that folder on to your service provider, or store it as a tidy archive of the project.

To package the files, select Package from the File menu. The Printing Instructions dialog box appears, providing a place for you to enter contact information and instructions related to the job. This is a great place to communicate with your service provider, or, if you've archiving the file, a good way to note the document's purpose and process. When you're finished adding information, click Continue.

In the Create Package Folder dialog box, name the folder to hold the files and specify where it should be saved. Then, for best results, select Copy Fonts, Copy Linked Graphics, and Update Linked Graphics in Package. To output the document correctly, all the fonts and graphics must be included; updating the linked graphics changes the links to point to the graphics in the folder, saving you from having to relink them later.

Click Package, and you're done! InDesign gathers all the files into a folder, ready to transfer to a service provider or an archive directory.

# Printing a File

**Print your document with the print settings that will give you the best results.**

## 1. Choose File > Print.

All the printing action takes place in the Print dialog box. When you've pre-flighted your document and corrected any problems, choose File > Print.

In the General pane of the Print dialog box, choose your printer **A**. If you're using a PostScript printer, make sure the appropriate PPD file is listed **B**. If the PPD file is incorrect, set up your printer driver with the correct PPD file. The PPD file gives InDesign information about your printer, including its printable area, installed fonts, and resolution.

The General pane also contains basic printing options. This is where you specify which pages to print—and which objects on the pages, such as nonprinting objects or guides.

The preview icon in the lower-left corner of the dialog box shows you how the page will print **C**. If you select Spreads, the preview changes to reflect that.

## 2. Select the Paper Size and Positioning Options.

When you created your document, you specified a page size and orientation for it. To ensure that it prints to the proper paper size, with the appropriate orientation, select the Setup pane. Then, choose the paper size and select an orientation. If the document is smaller or larger than the paper size you choose, select options for tiling or scaling the document.

## 3. Specify Marks, Bleeds, and Slugs.

Printer's marks include crop marks, which show the printer where to trim the document; bleed marks; registration marks; color bars; and page information, such as the document name and the date. You can print any combination or all of these marks. When you select a mark to print, the preview icon changes to show it. You can change the offset; generally, 3 mm is a good distance.

If you've included a bleed in your document, you can use the existing bleed settings in the document or customize the bleed settings for this printing. The bleed appears as a light pink area around the outside of the document in the preview icon. You can also include a slug area, which may provide additional information about the document.

Of course, in order to include printer's marks and bleeds, your paper size must be larger than your page size.

| Print | | |
|---|---|---|
| Print Preset: | [Custom] | |
| Printer: | Adobe PDF | |
| PPD: | Adobe PDF | |

General
Setup
Marks and Bleed
**Output**
Graphics
Colour Management
Advanced
Summary

**Output**

Colour: Separations    ☐ Text as Black

Trapping: Off

Flip: None    ☐ Negative

Screening: 71 lpi / 600 dpi

**Inks**

| | Ink | Frequency | Angle |
|---|---|---|---|
| | ▪ Process Cyan | 63.2456 | 71.5651 |
| | ▪ Process Magenta | 63.2456 | 18.4349 |
| | ▫ Process Yellow | 66.6667 | 0 |
| | ■ Process Black | 70.7107 | 45 |
| | ■ PANTONE 8281 C | 70.7107 | 45 |
| | ■ PANTONE 207 C | 70.7107 | 45 |

Frequency: 63.2456 lpi    ☐ Simulate Overprint

Angle: 71.5651 °    ( Ink Manager... )

( Page Setup... ) ( Printer... ) ( Save Preset... ) ( Cancel ) ( **Print** )

---

**INSIGHT**

**Spot Colors and Transparency.**
When you print a composite of a document that contains spot colors and transparency to a color printer, shaded squares may appear around some graphics. To prevent this, temporarily switch spot colors to process colors in the Ink Manager. Make sure to deselect All Spots to Process in the Ink Manager before printing color separations.

---

## 4. Set Up Inks for Printing.

If you're printing a color document, it's important that the inks print the way you expect them to. All of the color printing controls are on the Output pane of the Print dialog box.

First, from the Color menu, choose whether you're printing a composite or separations. Choose Composite CMYK or Composite RGB depending on the device you're printing to. Choose Composite Gray if you want to print the document to a black-and-white printer. Choose Separations to have color separations performed by InDesign as you print. Choose In-RIP Separations only if you are printing to a RIP (Raster Image Processor) that can perform color separations; this option is typically appropriate only if a service provider is printing the document.

If you're printing a composite, you needn't worry about the inks. However, if you're printing separations, check that the inks listed in the dialog box represent the separations you want to print.

You can make changes to the inks before printing. For example, you can convert spot colors to process colors if you want to print fewer plates. Click Ink Manager to make changes to inks. In the Ink Manager, select All Spots to Process to convert the spot colors to process colors. To make changes to an individual ink, select it and then change its type, neutral density, or trapping sequence. If you want to remap an ink to print on a different separation, select it and then choose an ink alias for it.

## Print

**Print Preset:** [Custom]
**Printer:** Adobe PDF
**PPD:** Adobe PDF

General
Setup
Marks and Bleed
Output
**Graphics**
Colour Management
Advanced
Summary

### Graphics

**Images**

Send Data: Optimised Subsampling

**Fonts**

Download: Complete
☑ Download PPD Fonts

PostScript®: Level 3
Data Format: ASCII

( Page Setup... ) ( Printer... ) ( Save Preset... ) ( Cancel ) ( **Print** )

## 5. Specify How Graphics and Fonts Will Print.

You can change the way graphics and fonts are downloaded to the printer, depending on your purpose. Select the Graphics pane to see your options.

If you're printing a quick proof of a document that has many high-resolution graphics, Optimized Subsampling is a good choice from the Send Data menu. If you're printing to a high-resolution printer for final output or creating a PDF file, choose All to ensure that InDesign sends all the data your device can use.

Usually, you'll want to choose Complete from the Download menu in the Fonts section of the dialog box. If you choose Subset, InDesign will send only the characters you actually used in the document. You may not need to download the fonts that are present on your printer; however, if you have any concerns that the PPD file may not be accurate for your printer, or that you may have used a different version of a font than is present on your printer, select Download PPD Fonts.

### Colour Management

**Print**

⦿ Document (Profile: Euroscale Coated v2)
○ Proof (Profile: N/A)

**Options**

Colour Handling: Let InDesign Determine Co...
Printer Profile: U.S. Web Coated (SWOP) v2

Output Colour: Separations
☑ Preserve CMYK Numbers
☐ Simulate Paper Colour

**Description**

Position the pointer over a heading to view a description.

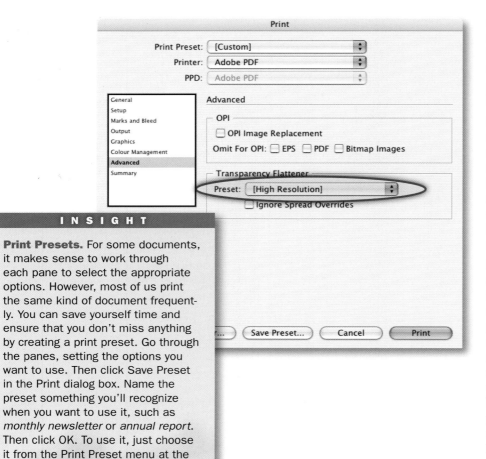

## 6. Set OPI and Transparency Flattener Options.

If you haven't used any transparency or OPI images, you can skip the Advanced pane. However, if you have, this pane becomes critical.

OPI (Open Prepress Interface) lets you use low-resolution images while you're designing your document, so that the screen refreshes and the file opens faster. Then, when you print your document, high-resolution images are substituted. If you're using OPI, select OPI Image Replacement and select the types of images that should be replaced.

Except for quick proofs, you should always be using the High Resolution transparency flattener style or a custom style that is designed for high-resolution printing. Remember that this style determines the resolution used to rasterize effects during flattening, and that it determines how much of your artwork will remain vector and how much will be rasterized. Even if you don't think you've used transparency in your document, it's a good idea to choose the High Resolution flattener style. Transparency can sneak into a document through drop shadows, feathering, and other effects.

## 7. Print!

When you've set all the options in all the panes in the Print dialog box, you're ready to go. Click Print. InDesign sends the file to the device you chose. If you are printing to an Adobe PDF printer, InDesign creates a PDF file. ▦

# Exporting a High-Quality PDF File

*Exporting a document to PDF is easy using the Export PDF dialog box in InDesign.*

**1. Choose File > Export.**

You could print a document to PDF using the Adobe PDF printer in the Print dialog box, but you have more control over the process if you export it. Options available in the Export dialog box are similar to those in Acrobat Distiller. Choose File > Export. Then, choose Adobe PDF for the format, name the file, and choose a folder for it. Click Save. The Export PDF dialog box appears.

## 2. Set the Basic Options for the PDF File.

On the General pane of the Export PDF dialog box, choose which pages you want to include, and whether you want to export them as individual pages or as spreads. If you're creating a magazine or book, consider exporting spreads to give the online reader the same experience as the physical reader.

Choose compatibility for the PDF file based on what your readers will be using and what you've included in the file. If you've embedded movie files or want to retain transparency, the file must be Acrobat 6 compatible. Otherwise, consider what your audience is likely to be using.

You typically don't need to embed thumbnails, which increase the size of the PDF file, because recent versions of Adobe Reader and Acrobat create thumbnails on the fly. However, be sure to select Bookmarks, Hyperlinks, and Interactive Elements if you want them to appear in your PDF file.

## 3. Choose Compression Options.

One of the benefits of PDF files is that they are smaller than other documents. How small they are depends on the compression options you choose. Select the Compression pane to set those options.

If you intend to print the PDF file to a high-resolution printer, set the compression options to provide high-resolution images. However, if you're going to post the PDF file online and don't expect people to print it to high-resolution devices, you can make the file much smaller by lowering the resolution significantly.

## 4. Select Other Options for Your PDF File.

If you're preparing a PDF file to pass on to a service provider or to show a client for proofing, you may want to include printer's marks and bleeds. Change those settings on the Marks and Bleeds pane.

If you're using color management, change settings for it on the Advanced pane. That's also where you'll find the Transparency Flattener option. As with printing, you'll almost always want to use the High Resolution flattener style. (Acrobat 6.0 supports transparency, so if you've chosen Acrobat 6.0 or later-compatibility, the transparency preset option is dimmed.)

You can set security options, including a password for opening the document, on the Security pane. This can be very important if you're working on confidential documents. You can also restrict whether readers can change the document, including copying text or extracting pages, if you're concerned about the use of copyrighted material.

## 5. Export the PDF File.

When you've set all the options, you're ready to export the PDF file. Click Export. InDesign creates the PDF file and, if you've selected "View PDF after Exporting" in the General pane, opens it in Adobe Reader or Acrobat.

It's a good idea to look through the PDF file to ensure that it includes all the pages, hyperlinks, bookmarks, and anything else you expect, before distributing it. █

### T I P

**PDF Presets.** If you create similar PDF files frequently, save time by using a preset. Set the options you want to use, and then click Save Preset at the bottom of the Export PDF dialog box. Give the preset a name you'll recognize later.

### I N S I G H T

**Choosing a Preset.** The presets that come with InDesign CS are quite useful. For multimedia PDF files, the Acrobat 6 Layered preset is a good choice, as long as you also select Hyperlinks and Interactive Elements on the General tab. For high-end printing, the Press preset is reliable, but you should communicate with your service provider about any specific settings it requires.

# Numbers and Symbols

## F

Feather dialog box, 147, 154
feathering, 147
fields, 163, 167, 168
File Browser, about, 26
File Information dialog box, 125
File Navigator workspace (Bridge), 29
files. *See also* importing; PDF files
    adding colored labels in Bridge, 30, 31
    checking information stored with, 125
    exporting PDF, 172, 173, 187–189
    importing text, 42–43, 121
    opening with button, 163
    organizing, 120
    packaging, 181
    pasting Adobe Illustrator, 129
    placing Photoshop, 135
    printing, 182–186
    showing information of image, 83
    working with in Bridge, 27
fill
    color of, 95, 103, 106
    dragging and dropping swatches for, 108
    making Fill icon active, 110
    overprinting, 115
    reversing values of stroke and, 54, 94
Fill icon, 110
Filmstrip Focus workspace (Bridge), 29
filtering documents, 31
Find Font dialog box, 69
finding
    fonts, 55, 69
    graphics in documents, 124
    InDesign palettes, 68
flattening transparencies, 175, 176, 177, 186
folder navigation in Bridge, 27
font styles, 55
fonts
    choosing text, 55
    default, 43
    finding, 55, 69
    preflighting, 179
    previewing, 55
    specifying printing of, 185
force justification, 50
formatting. *See also* Eyedropper tool
    Eyedropper tool for, 60–65, 93, 109
    paragraph styles, 62–63
    removing cell, 98
    removing from text before importing, 43

table text, 92
text, 54–59
Frame tool, 24
frames
    centering images in, 77
    color applied to text, 108
    columns within, 44
    converting clipping path to, 144
    creating, 42, 79
    cropping image, 97
    dragging and sizing, 122
    duplicating, 76
    fitting images to, 123
    hiding frame edges, 107
    placeholder, 75
    placing PDF file in, 127
    QuarkXpress vs. InDesign text, 69
    resizing content within, 22
    text, 24–25
    text insets, 44
    threading text in, 69, 80, 82
    vertical justification of text, 45

## G

General tab (Export PDF Options dialog box), 188
General tab (Print dialog box), 182
glow effect with drop shadows, 143
glyph scaling, 51
Glyphs palette, 59
Gradient icon, 112
Gradient Options dialog box, 113
Gradient palette, 113
gradients, 112–113, 144
graphics
    adding tables to, 96–97
    colorizing placed images, 133
    copying and pasting images, 132, 149
    cropping images, 97, 122, 127
    display quality of, 128
    displaying file information for, 83
    dragging and dropping into documents, 77
    fixed baselines, 99
    Links palette, 124–125
    pasting into table cells, 97
    Photoshop PDF files, 130–133
    placing images, 83, 119, 120–121
    placing PDF files, 126–127

positioning, 97, 122–123, 183
preflighting, 178, 179
preparing transparency output, 176–177
relinking, 124, 132
replacing for button state, 164–165
resizing, 123
rotating, 33
specifying printing of, 185
working with Illustrator and Photoshop, 128–129
grids
    aligning text to baseline, 46–47
    guides for, 75
    snapping text to, 47
guides, 75, 94

## H

H&J Violations option (Preferences dialog box), 52
Hand tool, 17
hanging punctuation outside margins, 53
hidden characters, 90
hiding
    contextual buttons, 166
    fields, 163, 168
    frame edges, 107
    guides, 94
hyperlinks, 158–159
Hyperlinks palette, 158
hyphenation, 52

## I

ICC color profiles, 34
icons
    Autoflow, 82
    dragging and dropping, 71, 84, 85
    Gradient, 112
    justification, 50
    loaded text, 43
    preview, 183
    reducing size of page, 87
    Swap Fill and Stroke, 110
    Swatches palette, 105
Illustrator. *See* Adobe Illustrator CS
Image Import Options dialog box, 121
images. *See* graphics
importing, 119–133